Ourselves as Students

The Broad Minds Collective

Kaaren Ancarrow
Nan Byrne
Jean Caggiano
Anita Clair Fellman
Brigita Martinson

Ourselves as Students

Multicultural
Voices
in the
Classroom

২৯

Compiled and Edited by
The Broad Minds Collective

Southern Illinois University Press
Carbondale and Edwardsville

Library of Congress Cataloging-in-Publication Data

Ourselves as students : multicultural voices in the
    classroom / compiled and edited by the Broad Minds
    Collective.
        p.   cm.
    Collection of essays written by students at Old Dominion
University.
    Includes bibliographical references (p.).
    1. Old Dominion University—Students—Attitudes. 2.
Multicultural education—United States—Case studies. 3. College
students—United States—Attitudes—Case studies. 4. College
students—United States—Social conditions—Case studies.   I.
Broad Minds Collective.
LD4331.087   1996
378.755'523—dc20
ISBN 0-8093-2087-8 (alk. paper)   96-15621
ISBN 0-8093-2088-6 (pbk : alk. paper)   CIP

The paper used in this publication meets the minimum
requirements of American National Standards for Information
Sciences – Permanence of Paper for Printed Library
Materials, ANSI Z39.48-1984. ⊚

Contents

Preface

We read and hear a good deal these days about the importance of multicultural education as the key to preparing us for
the workplace of the twenty-first century, for the global challenges facing us, and for the increasing diversity of our own
schools. Much of the attention has been directed toward the
curricular and pedagogical changes required for educational
multiculturalism with its goals of more inclusive course content and teaching techniques that will reach a greater variety
of students. Multiculturalism at the university level has mostly
focused on the hotly debated transformation of the curriculum,
on issues of access to postsecondary educational opportunities,
and on the need to diversify the demographic profile of university faculty.

Often missing from the discussion, however, even at the
university level, are the voices of the students themselves.
What are their responses to the culturally diverse classroom?
To the changes in curriculum? What impact—if any—do they
gauge their own race, class, gender, and ethnic identities to
have upon them as students? Under what conditions do they
feel they learn best? Do they perceive congruency between
their own culture and the university culture, and does this
affect their ability to learn? By the time young people are of
college age, they have had a wealth of experiences as students
and are aware, to varying degrees, of the role of cultural identity in their own and others' lives. What if they were asked to
ponder the overlap between their identity as students and
their gender, race, class, and ethnic identities?

This overlap is the starting point for *Ourselves as Students:
Multicultural Voices in the Classroom*. We have asked university
students from a variety of backgrounds to speak to readers

and to describe in their own words how and whether their cultural identities have affected their educational experiences. Our essayists are drawn from the student body of Old Dominion University, a large, urban school in Norfolk, Virginia. While we are fully aware that these fifty-eight essays do not reflect all the experiences of all American university students—or even all Old Dominion students—we do suspect that aspects of what these essayists say will strike a chord with most of their peers across the country.

Although not a household name, Old Dominion University (ODU) is, we believe, fairly typical of American universities in the 1990s. It is a state-assisted institution of sixteen to seventeen thousand students located in the center of a metropolitan region in eastern Virginia with a main campus and several satellite centers. (See appendix A for specific demographic information about the makeup of ODU's student body and faculty.) As is increasingly common across the country, most of its students do not live on campus, although a good many of them do live within a few miles of the university or one of its satellite centers. A hefty minority of its students attends school part-time, but even the full-time students are likely to hold part-time or full-time jobs or to have considerable domestic responsibilities in addition to their school work. With the recent introduction of TELETECHNET (instruction by television beamed to centers across the state), even more of ODU's students will experience the university in a nontraditional form.

ODU's students come from a variety of backgrounds. Generally speaking, it is fair to say that the university attracts a moderate number of minority (especially African-American) and international students, that men and women are evenly represented, and that its student body is somewhat older than the traditional college-age student. Some are the products of homogeneous communities—white or black—while others graduated from high schools that are more heterogeneous than ODU. Hence, some students have had considerable experience in multicultural environments, but for many, the university is the first setting in which they routinely have encountered people of other races, social classes, and nationalities. In terms of its cultural diversity and the political perspectives of members of the university community, ODU probably strikes a midpoint among other American colleges and universities.

Like most other American schools, and especially schools in the South, ODU is not the same institution it was a generation ago. Its student body is now more diverse as is its faculty and even its administrators and staff. In recent years, the university has tried to make the campus a more genuinely multicultural environment, rather than a place that simply happens to draw a number of minority as well as international, gay, lesbian, and disabled students, faculty, and staff. It has offered "Valuing Diversity" workshops for staff and faculty and has transformed its Minority Student Services Office into a Multicultural Student Services Office. This office serves gay, lesbian, and bisexual students, sponsors an annual Unity Week, and holds a series of workshops on diversity. The university has separate offices for disability services and for international students and faculty, has created an African-American Cultural Center, and offers a minor in African-American studies. A Filipino-American Cultural Center will open soon. The residence hall counselors receive training in dealing with a racially and culturally diverse student body and schedule programs for the residence halls that will increase multicultural awareness. While these efforts may have reduced the number of racial incidents on campus, they do not seem to have resulted in a discernible breaking down of barriers between groups. In terms of academic success, measured by graduation from the university, the numbers are virtually identical for African-American and white students, both of whom are more likely than members of other groups to finish an undergraduate degree at ODU.

Women occupied a marginal position on campus a generation ago. No longer. Now they are served by three distinct units and organizations: a women's center that offers noncredit classes, workshops, and community outreach; a strong watch-dog organization, the Women's Caucus; and a women's studies program that is the oldest in Virginia and the first among state-assisted universities to offer a baccalaureate in women's studies. The school is a national leader in providing sports opportunities and athletic scholarships for women. Nevertheless, the picture is not entirely rosy. Only recently have women attained the upper echelon of university administration, and women are unevenly distributed as full-time faculty members across the six colleges of the university. Female students are still sometimes treated with less respect and given less serious attention than their male peers, and some faculty members honor the requirement that all general education courses contain materials on women and minorities with a token lecture or reading assignment. The presence and uneven enforcement of a sexual harassment policy has not eliminated all incidents of harassment, especially those of the less blatant type.

Although ODU has the highest percentage of African-American faculty among Virginia schools that are not designated as historically black institutions, it is still likely that most current students will graduate from the university without ever having taken a class from an African-American, Hispanic, or Native-American professor; fewer will have missed being taught by a white female instructor. To diversify the faculty, ODU has implemented the President's Graduate Fellowship Program. This program recruits individuals from groups underrepresented in fields taught on campus and offers them financial support for terminal degrees in those fields in exchange for three years of employment with the university in tenure-track faculty positions.

This, then, is the institutional backdrop against which to place the student self-portraits contained in these pages. ODU has never managed to acquire a distinct identity for itself. It is not predominantly a "party school" or a place of fanatic loyalty to its athletic teams; it is not a university renowned for its superb library or its many famous professors or alumni; it does not boast a highly political student body. It is a good school but one to which students are free to assign their own characterizations in the absence of predetermined notions. Thus, some students gauge it to be fundamentally a working-class university, while others refer to the substantial number of well-off students. Students find it both a friendly and an inhospitable place. While many of them think of ODU as a commuter school, others, who live on or near campus, base their extracurricular and social lives around the school and their classmates. Minority students tend to refer to the university as a predominantly white institution, and white students view ODU as racially mixed. This fluidity of institutional identity may have contributed as well to the considerable range of responses on the part of our student essayists.

Ourselves as Students had its start as an assignment in a women's studies class at ODU in 1993. In order to explore the relationship between knowledge and knowledge seekers and to help students understand why certain topics and forms of knowledge were more compelling or alternatively, more intimidating to them than others, the students in the mixed undergraduate and graduate course were asked to write brief analyses of themselves as students. They were to account for the impact of gender, race, and social class on what they studied and what they heard in class. They were to examine how they were treated in the classroom and how they treated others there. They were to determine what their level of comfort was in the university. They were invited to consider variables such as religion, nationality, age, sexual orientation, or disability, if these were significant to their identities as students. They were urged to consider not only the disadvantages these various identities gave them, but also the privileges and advantages.

The resulting essays were remarkable in their eloquence, honesty, and thoughtfulness. With the students' permission, Anita Clair Fellman, the instructor, shared the essays, first within the class, and then with others on campus. Everyone who read those first seventeen essays was moved and fascinated. When does one ever get the opportunity to hear students acknowledging the ease with professors that a privileged class background gives them? Or to read of a black woman student's conclusion that her parents' efforts to shield her from the worst aspects of racism spurred her to become a lifelong learner as a form of defense? Or to discover that a working-class undergraduate had chosen to major in English because she had learned to be adept at translating texts that had no immediate connection with her life? If seventeen essays could produce such diversity, it was tempting to seek out more student self-portraits to see what patterns emerged.

A group of four female graduate students from the course volunteered to form a collective to work on a book of essays like the ones prepared for their class. At their request, Anita Fellman joined them. The newly formed Broad Minds Collective set itself the task of collecting essays from a wide spectrum of ODU students. (See appendix B for the project description and the release form that were given to students.) Our goal was not to collect a precisely representative sample of all categories of students on campus, but rather to try to convey the diversity that marked our student body. We tried to choose essays that highlighted individuals' earnest efforts to wrestle with the topics we raised, opting, where possible, for those with distinctive voices. Our agreement or disagreement with an author's point of view was not relevant to an essay's inclusion.

Although the essayists come from many disciplines, the finished collection is weighted toward the voices of women students. We did not design the project in that way, but we have concluded that women seemed already to have given the subject more thought than their male peers. Not only did we receive a smaller number of submissions from men, but the scope of experiences and opinions among the male students on the topics we raised was narrower than among their female counterparts. In making our selection, we have tried to reflect the range of perspectives expressed in all the essays, from the open-minded to the angry and defensive.

Working as a collective, we have done some editing of these essays, striving to keep as close as we possibly could to the spirit, content, and form of the originals. In most instances, the essays had been written on a voluntary basis for extra credit in a class or sometimes simply from interest on a student's part. Consequently, there were no mechanisms in place to assure revisions, and only thirteen of the essayists completed second or third drafts. To facilitate readability, we have corrected mistakes in spelling and the more glaring grammatical errors, and we have clarified ambiguous sentences. Our collective editorial hand was heaviest in regard to punctuation in an effort to enhance narrative flow. A fair number of students set their essays in a sociological context that reiterated the assumptions of the collection; our tendency was to pare away to the students' own stories, leaving implicit generalizations to the cumulative effect of the essays and explicit generalizations to the brief chapter introductions and to the conclusion. Each student was given the opportunity to read and approve or disapprove the edited version of his or her essay. Some essays carry their authors' real names, full or abbreviated, while others appear with initials only or with a pen name.

The essays themselves, rather than categories predetermined by research in multicultural education, dictate the organization of the book. Although most essays contain several overlapping themes, we detected four universal motifs—hence four chapters, each beginning with our brief introduction. In the chapter entitled "Cultural Perceptions and Assumptions," students show their awareness of how culturally defined categories affect education. In "Belonging and Alienation in the Classroom," they discuss the degree to which they feel as if they belong at ODU and their level of comfort in the classroom. The essays in chapter 3, "Making Sense of Our Lives Through Education," reveal students' use of education to learn more about the forces that have shaped them. "In Search of an Education" highlights students' active efforts to wrest what they feel they need from a college education.

Acknowledgments

Our first thanks go to the several hundred Old Dominion University students who thought about the questions we posed and wrote frank and probing autobiographical essays in response. We are also indebted to those ODU faculty who introduced the project in their classes and encouraged students to write essays. We are grateful that all fifty-eight students whose essays we wished to include in this book were willing—and often eager—to be represented in *Ourselves as Students: Multicultural Voices in the Classroom*.

Dr. JoAnn Gora, the Provost of Old Dominion University, has seen the value of this undertaking from the beginning and has been generous in her praise of it to all and sundry. Friends of Women's Studies, the community support group for ODU's Women's Studies Program, contributed to *Ourselves as Students* at several key stages. They underwrote the dramatization, by Rebecca Williams, of the essays into a play by the same name and subsidized the production of the play in several locales in eastern Virginia. The actors, Kaaren Ancarrow, Cathleen Butler, Jean Caggiano, Sharon Kaplan, Michelle Roberts, and Tara Whitehurst, brought the student voices to life. Rebecca Williams's dramatization pushed us to understand that our job as editors was to highlight the drama and narrative drive of the essays. As we were preparing the several drafts of this manuscript, Friends of Women's Studies again provided essential financial support. Dr. Maggi Curry-Williams, Associate Dean of Students, kindly read the introduction to help us avoid egregious errors of fact; she should not be held responsible for our interpretation of the university's policies. The Office of University Planning and Institutional Research at ODU helped us with some additional information that was not available in their annual statistical profile. Dr. Mona Danner of the Department of Sociology and Criminal Justice aided in the presentation of the statistics in appendix A.

Vivian Evett skillfully transformed pages in various stages of revision into a clean manuscript. Elaine Dawson of the Office of Research Services in the College of Arts and Letters, who is a word processor and manuscript preparer extraordinaire, produced all other versions of this manuscript, including the camera-ready copy.

Ourselves as Students

1

Cultural Perceptions and Assumptions

₹ะ

Introduction

When we asked students if we leave our gender, race, social class, religion, nationality, age, sexual orientation, and physical disability at the classroom door, most student essayists responded emphatically. They asserted—sometimes with regret—that cultural identities make a difference in university life. Their essays indicate that many of them were aware of their distinct social identities as early as elementary school. Students from a wide variety of backgrounds, it seems, were able to recognize at a young age that there were inconsistencies between what was valued and believed at home and what was considered important at school, whether it was the assumption that schooling came second to earning a living or that retention of national identity was more important than assimilating into the American melting pot.

In this chapter, students tell us how an awareness of their social identities has influenced their classroom experiences and encounters, how it influences what they learn and what they choose to study, and how it determines whether they feel comfortable or welcome at the university.

In many of these narratives, students share with us the intimate details of their personal struggles against the cultural stereotypes and misunderstandings that penetrate even an institution of higher education. We can see them both acknowledging their identification as members of culturally defined groups and claiming their unique identities as individuals. Yes, she is black, one woman writes, but to her that means growing up on extensive rural family acreage and going to school with white children. Another woman acknowledges that she is white but is baffled that this category presupposes Mayflower or plantation-owner ancestry.

Clearly, these categories of identity do not look the same from the inside as they do from the outside. Discomfort with the whole process of labeling is most apparent in the essays of several of the white males represented in this chapter. For two of these students in particular, whiteness and maleness are less categories of description or analysis than they are the bases on which other people unjustly label them as privileged individuals; they feel trapped in a group they believe to be unfairly under attack. Another white male is more ambivalent. He believes that he has been the victim of reverse discrimination but acknowledges that if he found himself suddenly in the position of a woman or a minority group member he would take the opportunities he sees being offered.

In their essays, the students ponder how their social identities have affected their educations. A female student from an Irish working-class family learned at school that "the realities of a working-class background" separated her "from her classmates, teachers, and her own academic aspirations." In her essay, she outlines how her position outside the cultural framework of the university has influenced her experiences and educational choices. A young black woman informs us in her essay that the male-dominated field of engineering demands that she "supersede everyone in order to complete an average assignment." An older gay student feels that classroom rules determine what is "acceptable" knowledge; he has learned that if he speaks out about gays or lesbians he will become "alienated from the mainstream . . . captive in an invisible cage." In these instances, students speak poignantly of expectations based on cultural assumptions of race, gender, and sexual orientation that allow little room to reconcile personal knowledge about self-worth and abilities with educational experience.

Reading the essays in this chapter brings us one step closer to learning about student perceptions by providing valuable insight into how students both interpret and understand behavior through their own cultural filters. This is particularly apparent in the essay, "A High Will to Achieve." For this Chinese student-essayist, difference is based on language. She ascribes her talent in math "to the fact that I do math better than I can utilize English." This understanding of difference provides her with a logical reason and an understanding of what she calls the American cultural stereotype that she is "a typical Chinese person who is gifted in math and logic." Her essay provides a look at how students are both affected by cultural assumptions and are participants in their creation.

All these essays offer information about how students understand their own culture and its assumptions, as well as how they perceive the current academic culture of our educational institutions. We learn from them that despite the new emphasis on multiculturalism, all too often the classroom response to the concept of difference is to view it as either problematic for the student or as peripheral to mainstream educational concerns. While some students are able to write about the advantages of assuming and accepting cultural expectations, many more, it appears, write about the coercive nature of educational institutions that demand that students become willing bridges between academic and nonacademic worlds.

਩

Earning a Living Always Came First

It is important to stand firm in the conviction that nothing can truly separate us from our pasts, when we nurture and cherish that connection.

—bell hooks

I come from a family of Irish; my parents were the children of Irish-Catholic immigrants. My mother and father were raised in the same working-class neighborhood in New York City. My father left school at sixteen to work carrying messages during the depression. My mother remained in school until tenth grade, when a defense job in a factory lured her away during World War II. When I was a child, these simple facts would startle me. It is only now, as I look back, that I realize that as a child I often wondered at what grade I, too, would be asked to leave school to help out. School and learning were extras; earning a living always came first.

I was raised in New York City and later on Long Island where my parents moved to escape their small apartment, the city crime, and the streets where we played, the same streets they ran as children. Before I went to school, I believed that everyone lived as we did—with Mass on Sunday, fish on Friday, one bathroom, two to a room, boys playing ball, girls cleaning up and washing. We were isolated in our ethnicity. In our neighborhood, fathers worked as city cops, repairmen, garbage collectors, or mechanics, some hourly jobs that took them into Brooklyn, Queens, or the city. Mothers had babies, "as many as God let them," and stayed home if their husbands demanded it or worked if they had no husband or one who wouldn't. I learned early from my religion, my parents, and my neighborhood my place in society. It was not until I reached school that I learned there were different rules for each race, class, sex, and ethnic group.

It was at school that I would learn about the realities of my working-class background and how it would separate me from my classmates, teachers, and my own academic aspirations. School taught me about the desire to belong and about the politics of economic exclusion. These lessons in ambivalence taught in the classroom I bring to everything I do.

The economic realities of my life always provided the boundaries of my education, drawing a sharp line between my dreams for myself and what I was actually expected to accomplish. I have always felt that anything I have been able to accomplish was due more to luck and circumstances and my will to survive than it was to any ability I had or resources my mother and father could provide.

As a child growing up and later as a young woman in college, I believed that the classroom revolved around money—that I could not learn without resources—money for milk, school pictures, and field trips at first. Later, money for books, transportation, and supplies. The simple fact that for some children there would always be money for classroom "necessities" was something I learned at school. It was not until I had earned enough money to support myself that I realized that class was more than just money—it was a boundary.

I attended a state university on an academic scholarship, and I remember quite clearly how I felt in one of my first college courses when I heard the comments of my French professor about the requirements for majoring in foreign language. My professor maintained that students who wanted to learn foreign language could never truly be "prepared" for college-level study without traveling abroad. I, who could barely afford the living expenses at the university, was excluded, for I knew I could sooner have danced on the moon than studied abroad. His perspective became the norm of study in that classroom, and I knew that even after five years of study in high school, college-level French study would be closed off to me. The classroom seems to be built around this type of inequality, an inequality constructed by assumptions.

The influence of gender on my classroom experience is not to be ignored. If I were asked, I would be compelled to name my femaleness as having the most significant impact on my formal education. My perspective on my gender was shaped by the rigid exclusionary policies practiced by my church and the school system in which I was educated. My school enforced a rigid dress code for female students, provided a second-rate athletic program for girls, and actively advised young women away from math and science courses. My religion acknowledged my womanhood with a white dress at communion and a slap in the face at confirmation. I was obliged to cover my head with a hat or veil, hope for a son who would become a priest, and was often reminded that children were a gift from God over which women would have no control. From my church, I learned about being a woman with the power to create, but I also learned of my own powerlessness.

My own powerlessness as a woman is something that sits in every classroom with me. It keeps me quiet when men talk; it jumps me to my feet when someone needs something; and it calms me when I fail. This is difficult for me to acknowledge.

I feel not only powerless in the classroom, but passive. My discomfort with discussion is real; although I feel naturally inclined to learn from other students through a shared experience, I sometimes think I have little of value to say. I am like many other women who have never felt our ideas or thoughts were taken seriously in the classroom—I am uncomfortable hearing myself speak.

This year, though, I feel like I have come full circle. I am back in the classroom, and I bring new expectations, but I come knowing that I am still connected to my past.

—Nan Byrne

A High Will to Achieve

I am an oriental female student who has had most of my schooling in Shanghai, China. In the Chinese culture, there is always hope among families to bear a son and not a daughter because a daughter cannot carry on the family name. Population is also a serious problem in China, and each family may only have one child. Therefore, I am an only child and have acquired certain qualities that differentiate me from other females. I am a bit tomboyish and have a high will to achieve.

After I was born, my family was mostly a one-parent family because my father spent the majority of his time on the national aviation team in Shanghai. During my father's absences, my mother worked very hard for our survival. I felt I had to assume the male role of being strong and unyielding to protect her from harm. I remember one instance in which a neighbor bullied my mother in the residents' kitchen. During that time, there was only one kitchen to an apartment complex. I could not bear the sight of her bullying my mother and rebelled even though it was not right to speak to an elder in such a tone. My background has taught me to be independent in all facets of life. It also contributes to my continuing perseverance in education.

I believe that my race has an effect on the way I react in the classroom. In China, it is very difficult to enter a university because there are so many people, yet so few educational institutions. In order to be admitted, one has to be a superior student. Failure usually translates into a life of hard labor. Some people commit suicide because they are not admitted to one of the few universities. Shanghai is not like the United States, where even the average student may attend a suitable university. I had to constantly battle this fear of failure in the classroom. Fortunately, I was admitted to the University of Shanghai and later was able to come to the United States to study with the support of my relatives in Hong Kong. I had decided to come to the United States to study and to be better than the average Shanghai student and have a better future. This view of hard work by our race has helped me to excel.

Our family in Shanghai is considered upper middle class as a result of years of consistent hard work. My mother is a doctor, and my father is a professional coach. In Shanghai, a majority of my friends are in the same social class and are all well educated. It is these friends, my peers, who encouraged me to do well in school. Most were very active and all had high grade-point averages. I think that these friends have also had a great impact on my view of the importance of education.

Upon attending Old Dominion University, I have found that my social experience and the identities I assumed in the past in China have contributed considerably to my academic progress in the United States. Being away from my home country, my need to be successful and not fail is greater. The only barrier in my major field of study is one of language. Classes containing mathematical problem solving appeal to me more than classes such as systems analysis, which require understanding of complex terminology. This weakness makes courses containing mathematics and logic more interesting. I remember taking a class in a computer language where these two factors were prevalent, and as a result, I did exceptionally well. This is probably the reason why so many American students stereotype me as a typical Chinese person who is viewed as being gifted in math and logic. The truth lies more in the fact that I do math better than I can utilize English. I am mostly silent in class due to the same problem, but I usually talk to the instructor on a one-to-one basis after class. I try to listen, but a majority of the time I cannot understand because of the fast pace at which the instructor speaks. Therefore, I must spend an enormous amount of time reading the book with the aid of my English-Chinese dictionary. In spite of all this, I still do well in all my courses. Even though it is very difficult for me to study in the United States, I must study hard and be successful in order to fulfill my parents' and peers' hopes. Therefore, I bring all the hopes, social experiences, and identities into the classroom.

—Ling Ling

I've Always Felt As If I Belong

As I continue my education through every class of every year of every school, I am aware of three specific aspects of my identity: older, white, and male. The least consequential of these is my maleness. One of my misconceptions upon returning to school was that business administration, specifically the accounting field, is a typically male-dominated industry. In actuality, my accounting classes seem to be female dominated. I don't have any problem with this; it is just contrary to what I had previously believed. I haven't noticed any difference in the teaching practices or in my own ability to feel comfortable with the material.

One part of my identity that helps me feel more comfortable with my classes is my race—Caucasian. I had never previously considered how much I take this for granted until I encountered a particular member of a racial minority in several of my classes. This man would always arrive last, sit in the very back, and never offer any input to the lectures. It was not until we had a class with several of his friends that I realized he was not shy. I can only speculate that the reason for his silence was a feeling of not belonging. I have always felt comfortable enough with my surroundings to sit where I want and to speak in class. Since many instructors regard class participation as worthy of credit, I could say I've benefited because I've always felt as though I belong. Because I was raised in an all-white town, attended an all-white high school, and attended mostly white colleges and universities, my knowledge of black cultures and histories has been severely neglected.

Being an "older" student has had the most profound effect on my schooling. When I was younger and attended Penn State, someone was always looking to form a study group. The same was true when I attended Tidewater Community College, where the average age of the student body is twenty-nine. But no one has asked me to study with them since I entered ODU. I can only attribute this to my age. Now, I study more on my own, and it makes the learning process harder. In contrast, being older is a barrier to such distractions as partying. The bottom line is that being older makes it harder to feel as though I belong to the academic community.

Being older, white, and male has its advantages and disadvantages. My advantages could be construed as someone else's disadvantages. One thing I have learned is that I may make others feel uncomfortable without any knowledge or intention of doing so.

—B. W. S.

Proud of My Nationality

I am a twenty-one-year-old Palestinian woman attending Old Dominion University. Being the first girl in my immediate family to attend college is stressful at times. I have two brothers, one older and one younger, and a sister who is married with two sons. I live with my parents and my brothers. My father owns his own business, and my mother is a housewife. My family is very close knit.

Being female in a university does have an effect on me in the classroom. Gender bias cannot be blamed on the university, though; I believe it began when I entered elementary school. At the time, the boys in the classroom seemed to get more attention from the teacher than the girls. This led me to become reluctant to ask questions in the classroom. Throughout my education, some teachers made fun of inquiries from students. Now, with maturity and good, influential teachers, I'm overcoming this fear of being wrong. In college, more professors tell students that it's all right to ask questions, that there is no such thing as a stupid question. Such professors have boosted students' morale, perhaps without even realizing it.

I spent the first twelve years of my life in America. My parents taught us to always be proud of our nationality. I realized that I was different from the other children in school. My parents taught me that this difference was something special that no one could ever take away from me.

When I was thirteen, my family returned to Bir Nabala, a small town near Jerusalem, in the Occupied West Bank. This was once known, and still is to me and my people, as Palestine. Being young and naive, I didn't realize what was happening to my country. After we settled down and built a house, I started to like it there. Meeting new friends at the Quaker Friends School in Ramallah helped me through that difficult transition. Since it was a private school for girls, I did not experience any kind of gender discrimination. Actually, these were the only years in my education in which I felt very comfortable. There, I was allowed the freedom to express pride in my nationality.

This freedom was taken away from me on December 9, 1987. That is the date on which the Palestinian uprising known as the Intifada, began. By the end of December, all schools in the Occupied West Bank and Gaza Strip were closed. Our world and my dreams began to shatter. Schools, to this day, are still not operating on full schedule. My younger brother and I were the ones in my family who were most affected. The closure was devastating as well as frustrating for my family. Realizing this was happening to us because we were Palestinians infuriated us. The Israeli government was punishing us and trying to force us to become a people of ignorance.

Two and a half years had passed without an education when my father moved us back to the United States. It was a shock to me since I had not been back for five years. I was a senior in high school; thank God I passed a test and didn't have to repeat the years I missed, but still, knowing that those missed years could never be replaced was frustrating.

High school was so different in the United States. It was co-educational, and I had to struggle to keep up with my class. Many students couldn't understand the enormous pride I felt for my people. I noticed that nationalism didn't seem as important to most Americans. I believe this is true because most Americans feel secure and have a country, unlike the

Cultural Perceptions and Assumptions

Palestinians. Most of my teachers allowed me to make presentations on the ongoing problem in my homeland, which helped me cope a little more easily.

I'm glad for the opportunity that I've been given by my family to continue my schooling in America. It's a nice feeling to realize what freedom is. It's true that people don't recognize what they're missing unless it's been taken away from them. I am determined to finish my education and to return to my homeland to help the children there with the key to their future: education.

—Haifa Omar Jawhar

Learning in the Invisible Cage

When I walk into a classroom, I do not feel like a member of that class or a member of the common good. The cause of this is the perceived or real continued mistreatment and denial of my inalienable rights. I classify myself as a gay man (my exact orientation is bisexual). I am a gay veteran, an American. I know from my experiences that if I speak out against stereotypes of gays or lesbians that I will become alienated from the mainstream in the classroom. In high school, a rumor began that I was gay, and I watched people turn their backs on me. Former friends no longer associated with me; the teachers would not treat my questions as if they mattered. For a gay man or a lesbian woman to fully disclose their orientation is to invite hatred. From this unwillingness to be hated and irrationally feared we remain silent; we remain captive in the invisible cage. We refuse to allow ourselves to participate in order to avoid being discriminated against.

Some of the unfortunate effects of our silence are that stereotypes continue to be propagated. When we hear comments like "all faggots should have their heads cut off" (a paraphrase of a comment I heard in a class), an invisible bar is put up around us. When someone judges us on what they think we are instead of who we really are, a bar goes up. Very soon we are caged by the invisible barriers of misunderstanding and mutual distrust, and in that cage we all are prevented from knowing the true value of each person we meet.

From initial prejudices and misunderstanding come other

effects besides those manifested in the classroom. The psychological effects of being dehumanized by hate speech and the villainization of gays by the mass media eventually diminish a person's belief in herself or himself. It does not end there. It can also lead to a complete lack of faith and disillusionment in one's country. The hatred of any minority must soon end or the very nation we have all built and defended will collapse. There is perhaps only one road for us to take: the road of full participation of everyone for a just, democratic society. Through a united effort we may all come to understand we are more similar than dissimilar. As the pledge of allegiance tells us: "One nation under God, with liberty and justice for all."

In the men's room in the College of Arts and Letters, I saw scribbled in black marker the words, "All fags must die!" It reminded me of when I was in the Navy, and a shipmate, a person I had a very professional working relationship with, suddenly got the impulse to strangle me one night at the enlisted club in Naples, Italy. I recall his hands around my neck like a steel cage. I lay there, pinned to the floor, his legs trapping my chest. His visceral and sadistic words still remain in my mind, "I'm going to kill you, commie fag!"

I still feel the trap and pressure from that moment. Everyday in class I hear the same hate words, the same hatred and intolerance manifested in many different ways, subtle and overt. Why should gay or bisexual students have to feel that they are learning in an invisible cage? Why should we have to feel that it is impossible for us to fully participate in the learning environment of the university?

All of us are impaired in some way. There is always something that makes us reticent to speak and express ourselves, whether it is a prejudice of race, class, religion, or any other of a myriad of reasons. My concerns are those specific to the gay, lesbian, and bisexual student. Participation, as I define it, is the ability to speak freely and honestly about one's opinions, convictions, and faith in an open discussion.

—Michael McCarron

Society Tells Me That I Am White

I am a single, white female attending Old Dominion

University. I am a senior majoring in English with a journalism emphasis. The majority of the students in my journalism classes are male. Fortunately, I did not feel that certain major fields of study at Old Dominion University were closed off to me because of my gender, race, or class. I changed my major three times, going from business administration to art to English. Each department was more than supportive and seemed to welcome me with open arms. I felt very comfortable. I was drawn to women's studies courses, however, because of my gender. This is apparent when observing any of the women's studies classes at Old Dominion; the students are predominantly female.

Another class that I chose because of my gender was "Literature of the Developing World." It gave some very good insights into the lives that people from other parts of the world lead. After reading many of these novels, one finds that the lives of people in the developing world are not quite as different as we think.

Although I can identify with the writings and philosophies of minority writers, I am often told that I cannot really know what they are thinking or how they feel because I am white. This disturbs me very much. And why should my understanding of certain subjects depend upon my gender? Why should women feel hesitant about breaking into the "man's world of engineering," or the "male-dominated world of politics?" What should it matter? Understanding comes from within. It has nothing to do with the outer shell of the human body.

Sometimes I struggle with my own identity. Society tells me that I am white. I am not ashamed of the white race, but I feel like I am in some ways slighting my true ethnic heritage. I am not a white Anglo-Saxon Protestant, but a white European Catholic. My parents did not come to America on the Mayflower, and none of my ancestors ever lived in, or anywhere near, England. My father's grandparents immigrated to the United States in the late 1800s; my mother immigrated in 1962.

The society in which I have been raised is full of harmful stereotypes. Whenever I check "white" in the box on any form that asks what my race is, a whole identity goes along with my little check mark. It is assumed that I come from a privileged background and that my ancestors were Pilgrims or plantation owners. It is also assumed that I am a fair-skinned, blonde-haired, blue-eyed woman. I am actually brown-eyed, brown-haired, and olive-skinned. My family may be from Europe, but until another box is created for my specific ethnic group, I will still be called "white."

It is unfortunate that so many people hold me and other white individuals accountable for the mistakes of the past. My ancestors were not even living in the United States during the time of slavery. But besides that, we do not live in the past. We just need to try to make sure that it is not repeated. No one should feel that he or she needs to be silent in certain conversations because he or she does not have ancestors who were slaves or because he or she does not have ancestors who came to America on the Mayflower. America is a melting pot. It is made up of a mixture of many great races and ethnicities, but we all have one thing in common: we are all Americans. We should all feel equal, and we should all feel as if we "belong."

One of the reasons that I feel that I "belong" at Old Dominion University is because of my class background. I am lucky enough to come from a privileged background. College was always expected to be a part of my life. In December, I will be the last of four children who will receive a college degree. If my parents were not financially secure, things would probably be different. I would have had to work twice as hard so I could get some kind of financial assistance. Luckily, I was never faced with this dilemma.

I can't say what it would be like to be the only woman in an engineering class, or the only African American in a sociology class, because I have never been either. I do know that no one likes to be the outcast or the one who just doesn't blend in. Sometimes being generic is such a blessing.

—Marian Del Donna

Turning Disadvantages to Advantages

Born in 1970, I was raised in Woodside, Delaware. Delaware is a predominantly white state. Since my parents raised us in an unbiased area, racial prejudice was one topic I did not know much about. My "neighborhood" was the 500 acres owned by members of my father's family, so we played close to home. The high school that I went to was also predominantly white. I was accustomed to being in classrooms where there were only one or two black students. It really did not bother me. I normally operated well with other students, no matter what their race. I do not remember experiencing any racial tension among the faculty, staff, or students.

When I began to search for colleges, I started feeling the need to be around people of my own racial background. I do not know why I felt this way. I guess I felt the need for a change. At first, I looked at Howard University. It had the major I desired, it was away from home, and, most of all, it was predominantly black. My parents and relatives became fearful of such a drastic change from country to city life. After much discouragement from my family, I decided not to pursue a degree there. My next choice, because of the major I was seeking, was Old Dominion University. This was when I began to see the first signs of racial preferences among my family. They asked questions like, "Why didn't you try Norfolk State?" "Did you look into Hampton University?" and "Don't you see any black universities you want to go to?" I did not question my relatives when they asked me these questions. I assumed they felt I would be more comfortable at a black university. I know a couple of them felt that black students should attend a black university to support their own race. My reply to all of these questions was simply, "It has the major I am looking for in the perfect area (medium-sized city), in spite of the predominant race." Now I know I made the right choice.

However, many things became clear to me after I entered college. I joined a group called Fellowship of Minority Engineers and Scientists (FMES). They began talking about racial tension on campus, racial prejudice in the classroom, and the lack of black history in our history books. I began to gain perspective on some of my previous experiences. I did not develop hostile attitudes; on the other hand, I began to think. I became thankful for my former situation at home. The environment I was raised in had taught me that being a minority did not always have negative consequences. When I accepted being a minority, within myself, I did not accept failure or defeat but gained another reason to achieve the goals I had set for myself. The forums sponsored by FMES enlightened me to the fact that racial prejudice was still very much a part of our society—despite my more fortunate early experience.

My consciousness of the social-class factor also developed after entering college. I really began to feel that my parents were not wealthy enough to keep me in this university. I began to notice the expensive vehicles driven by students. The interesting part of this is that I was not treated any differently because I did not meet the social standard of many students. However, I felt inferior to many of my friends because of the way they dressed, acted, and talked. Students from all racial groups seemed to have the things I wished I had. Most of the time it was just the way I felt, not the way people made me feel. I remember one specific time when I was among friends sharing family backgrounds. Several people were talking about how their mothers and fathers had graduated from high school and gone to college and become someone really important. I did not have any trouble telling them that my mom was a nurse. But, I have to admit, I was ashamed to tell them my father was a custodian and had never gone to college.

I was fearful that conversations like this might arise in the classroom. That never happened; if it had, I do not know how I would have responded. This feeling of social inferiority definitely made me feel uncomfortable at the university. This experience has not lasted my entire five years here, but it was a factor in the first two. During that time, I found myself watching to see what type of lifestyle my friends were living and comparing it with mine. This began to put a strain on my friendships, so I made up my mind that I would get over this, and eventually, I did. Now it does not affect me, and I can be friends with the poorest person as well as the richest person. I am who I am, and I should be proud of that.

This brings me to the factor of gender. I have always loved being a female. However, because of my closeness to my father, "women's professions" bored me. I felt that a "man's job" was always more exciting and more challenging. In my childhood, I had several conversations with my father about the way electrical devices were made. My interest was sparked when I observed him fixing things and connecting wires and making our house electrically advanced. Although my father never attended a university, he has always been intelligent in the field of electronics. Early on, my father purchased a computer. I was fascinated, and so was he. We learned together how to use it and manipulate it for many things. I decided then to become an engineer. At the time I decided on this major, I loved computers but I loved the inside more than the outside. I decided I wanted to fix them. I was naive again, because I did not realize what I was actually about to embark upon. I entered a male-dominated field of study.

This did not become apparent to me until I entered college. In the beginning, it was no problem. It was when I began taking more advanced classes that I began to see what hardship I would have to endure because of my gender. When we worked in groups, I could never perform well enough or fast enough to stay abreast of our labs. This was not true in my eyes, but within the group, I felt tension and pressure to supersede everyone in order to complete the average assignment. Meetings among the male students were held without my knowledge, where work in which I was not included would be accomplished. It is frustrating to know that because I am a woman, I am looked on as inferior in a male-dominated profession. Even teachers have given me that impression. One professor in particular made the statement, "Most of you will get A's in here—even you, B——." How am I supposed to take a statement like that, especially if I am the only black female in the course? How has this made me feel? I do not feel that it is fair, but life is not fair. I have to work that much harder to prove that I can be a strong black woman and be an above-average engineer.

Although many of these situations have been uncomfortable, they have made me a strong person. I have used those things regarded by society as disadvantages to my advantage. To put this bluntly, I am a better person because I am a black woman raised in a lower-middle-class family. This does not mean that people who are not black, women, or raised in lower-middle-class families are less than I am. It just means that I have learned to be happy and satisfied in whatever situation I find myself.

—Blessed

I Would Do the Same Thing
If I Were in Their Position

Many people in my generation have been raised to think of every individual as equal regardless of gender, race, religion, and so on. As a twenty-one-year-old junior in college, I have found that such equality is lacking, if not absent altogether. Most people would probably agree that much of the discrimination today is against groups such as blacks and women. However, I have been discriminated against, as a white male, to the benefit of these groups.

The drive over the past thirty years for the rights of minorities has made those of us in the majority (white male) the indirect targets of reverse discrimination. I stress that this discrimination is INDIRECT in that it is ONLY a result of a push for the rights of the minorities. I first became aware of this discrimination when I was in high school and applying to colleges. I found that my higher SAT scores and leadership positions were not enough to win acceptance to a particular college. A few of my close friends, black males and females, were accepted to universities that I was not, even though I was more qualified (i.e., higher SAT, higher GPA). This provoked a certain amount of resentment, though I was not sure whom to be resentful toward—my friends for being who they were, or the "system" for making what I thought was a mistake.

When I entered the university, I was pulled toward the area of study that is still my major—criminal justice. However, I soon learned that getting good grades did not necessarily mean that I would get a job. I was told from the beginning that organizations such as city police forces have a great need for black and female officers. When I begin to apply for jobs in the criminal justice field, I may be secondary to such groups. I can only concentrate on my schooling to better my chances.

I have found it important, however, to regard such situations from the minority perspective. If I were a member of a minority group, I would, without a doubt, take advantage of any chances I might be given. I have talked to many students in my college courses who are doing just that. For instance, numerous minority individuals in my criminal justice courses are already planning to go on to the graduate level simply because they are underrepresented in master's and doctorate programs. I always offer them my wholehearted support because I would do the same thing if I were in their position.

Though I feel I am not given the same advantages in some situations as certain minority groups in my field, I do not feel like I am directly discriminated against. If anyone is directly discriminated against, it is the members of these minority groups. I have recognized that the majority of the material I study comes from a white male perspective. Therefore, I enrolled in the one criminal justice class offered on campus that provided a minority viewpoint and was taught by a black female. Classes like these, which offer a minority perspective, should be offered in all fields of study and should be required for graduation. Such classes enable individuals in the majority to better understand minority groups.

—A. L.

Personal Scholarly Baggage

Persecution starts at an early age. When I was five years old, I could have cared less if my classmates were black/white, Lutheran/agnostic, gay/straight, or whatever. I was very concerned that I was almost always last whenever roll was called. As far as last names go, Van Slyke did not lend itself to be in the front of the lunch line very often. It was hardly a coincidence that my best friend's name when I was that age began with a Z. We knew that we were in it together and had to bond against the early- and middle-namers. No, I'm not going to lecture anyone on the status of last names, that stratification has long been dismissed in this world of academics. My point is that as early as age five I was dealing with personal scholarly baggage. If this is true (and I assure you that it is—I have the mental scars to prove it), the baggage must multiply as we get older and gather more suitcases.

Ever since those days of kindergarten, the first day of class has always been my favorite, simply because it is the day all the parameters are set. The class definition is there, the syllabus is distributed, but most importantly, I find out who is in my class. This environment, established by the professor but maintained by the students, is what has excited me about learning in the classroom. But what happens when I walk into a classroom and I am not merely viewed as a student or as an English graduate student, but as a white, male, middle-class, American, heterosexual, underachieving, mid-twenties slacker?

I can't think of a time when I've ever been branded with all these categories at once, but I have felt the glances and attitudes of those who think that these categories are who I am. I have always been aware that most of my fellow English students have been female (undergraduate and graduate). It wasn't until I reached the graduate level that I ever realized that this was a problem. It seems to me that some female students have marked their territory. Recently, I have been advised not to take a certain course because I would be the only male in the classroom and that would "upset the balance." Upset the balance? I didn't say anything at the time simply because I was so shocked that someone would actually say that. What balance can there be if there is only one category of students in the class? I don't care if the class is being taught by a purple, androgynous, Nazi Hindu who can only hear consonants; a variety of student perspectives is essential in a classroom.

I do not want to argue the merits or demerits of feminism or any other cultural perspective. Feminists have many valid points, but why does it sometimes feel like I, simply because of my gender, am made to feel like a villain? Too often, if a classroom discussion turns to a female issue and the males have yet to speak out on the subject, a woman (or women) will demand to hear "what the men think." I do want to thank them for desiring all opinions, but I have never witnessed a conversation dominated by men where a man (or men) has turned to a woman in class and asked to hear her opinion. This is not because the men refuse to seek other perspectives. It is because the gender ratios in graduate-level English classes don't allow conversations to be dominated by men.

Men are simply outnumbered and outvoiced. It has gotten to the point where I almost feel I should try to apologize for the transgressors of the past who have wielded a phallus. Will

I apologize? No. They are not me and I am not them. I will not apologize for someone simply because we share a body part. In my eyes, women and men are equal. I have always thought that way. I just desire to be able to walk into a classroom and not be branded by what is between my legs but by what is between my ears.

—James Van Slyke III

See Me, Not My Clothes

We have all stared at people entering a classroom because they looked different. Differences could be color, gender, physical handicap, age, appearance, or anything else that made the person stand out from the norm. I am a twenty-one-year-old black male and a NROTC midshipman, and I feel that these are the most dominant characteristics that people notice about me when I walk into a classroom for the first time.

I am required to wear my uniform on Tuesdays, and this is when I notice the different reactions. On that day, I come into my classes and people look at me differently than when I walk into class on Thursdays. On Thursdays, I wear civilian clothing. Most of my civilian clothing is similar to that of a hoodlum. I like to wear loose-fitting, baggy jeans, hooded sweatshirts, sweat suits, tennis shoes, fitted baseball caps, and other things that "hoods" wear. When I am in uniform, I guess people see the uniform and not me. When I am in civilian clothing, I guess people see me and the "hoodlum" clothing. While I am in uniform, people are more friendly and considerate to me in and out of the classroom. For example, people I do not know will sometimes hold doors open for me and give me friendly greetings. When I am out of uniform, some people, who I do not know, are less likely to engage in a friendly conversation, and they also try to isolate themselves from me.

At first, these situations used to bother me. I did not know what people in class thought about me when I was in uniform and when I was not in uniform. I have heard people in class make comments about my civilian attire as if to question whether or not I was "fit" to wear the uniform. I figure that "it is the person who makes the clothes and not the clothes that make the person." In my opinion, people should be judged by what they are capable of doing and not by what they wear. We all have stereotyped and prejudged people, but we should not base our final judgment of people on their physical appearance.

As a young black male, I have noticed that people of other races tend to watch what they say around me. For example, any type of "black issue" that is talked about in the classroom is usually discussed in a very discreet manner so as to not offend or arouse any of the black students.

When I was in high school, I was urged to take a lot of math and science courses that dealt with engineering. I was not a genius in these courses, but I had people telling me to stick with engineering because I was a good student and a black male. At that time, I did not know what they meant. Now that I am older, I understand better. I have a serious problem with this type of counseling, which has placed me into certain classes and programs. Am I here because of what I can do, or am I here because of who I am? This sometimes causes me to doubt myself and my abilities.

—V. H. S.

Both Sides Now

I believe that who I am as a person—who I have been socialized to be—has had a great deal to do with my educational experiences. I enrolled in the ODU graduate sociology program mainly because I was offered an assistantship, although I actually had little information about the program. I was a bit apprehensive when I learned, after accepting, that it was a joint program with Norfolk State, a historically black university. I had never been to Norfolk State, and I really feared being in the racial minority. The adjustment did not come easily. The first year I spent most of my energy figuring out how to transfer to another program. Slowly, I began to realize that some of my fears and feelings of being unwanted at NSU were self-imposed, and others were founded in actual situations. I was suddenly aware of what it must feel like to always be considered the minority. I felt left out, unwanted, unable to identify with the other students, sometimes disliked for no reason. I still find myself sometimes walking with my head down at NSU.

I must say that this has been an invaluable growth experience that I am now thankful to have had. I wish that every white student could experience such a feeling, although I know that everyone in my program does not share my perspective. Some students have become hostile, and I do sympathize because there have been some ugly incidents. But I believe that the decision to focus in my thesis on some of the unique experiences of black women has come directly out of my understanding of the pressure that any majority puts on the perceived minority—and of course, in our society, black women have a double "curse."

In my graduate program, I have seen direct gender bias (with preferential treatment given to females in one class, based only on gender) and social class bias as well. What I realized from the things that I have witnessed and experienced is that the teacher's perception has more to do with the student's success than anything else. The teacher has the power to make or break a student at will and also to guide each student's performance with praise or criticism. I would never have believed the power of the teacher's bias if I had not seen it for myself. It is not a pleasant reality to see that one person can push you to do your best or so easily make you think that you are not capable of graduate work. I have experienced both, firsthand, and my confidence in myself has wavered, based on teacher approval or disapproval, whether it was warranted or not.

As a graduate teaching assistant, I have been able to experience the other side of the teacher-student relationship. It is all too easy to see more potential in certain students and to develop more interaction with those students, thus enhancing their learning. I have noted that my own biases were not based on race or gender (for the most part) but were usually based on personality and interest in topics. I am attempting to work more with students who seem uninvolved, for whatever reason, in order to avoid any possible bias that I may have.

In graduate school I have also found my own creativity. At last I realize that I have always been creative, but because no one ever acknowledged this, I feared any activity dealing with imagination, brainstorming, or art. Now I take pride in my own ability, mainly because people have taken the time to acknowledge that side of me.

—L. C.

A Practicing Wiccan: A Definite Minority

As a woman, school is a bit different for me than it is for the men for whom academic life was designed. Although my mother worked hard to insure that I did not reject courses of study because I was female, my gender did draw me to certain courses. For example, I chose to take a class in marriage and family dynamics because I believed, at least unconsciously, that it would be my responsibility to insure the healthy development of my future family. As a drama student, I chose to study scenography over costume design or stage management because it was *not* expected—a sort of mini-rebellion. Now I am taking women's studies in an attempt to make sense of the experiences I have had as a woman in a man's world. I find that the actions and works of women are sorely underrepresented in history and literature classes.

In class, I tend to resist both direct and subtle gender roles and male supremacy, and I consider myself to be more open than most people to feminist ideals. I tend to learn best in small and/or mostly female groups where I feel free to express my ideas. Often in larger classes, my culturally encouraged hesitation to interrupt inhibits my ability to join conversations with those who have no such compunctions. Some instructors have encouraged me in literature, grammar, and language, while others have discouraged me in math and physical education. I am not sure what, if any, effect this has had on my pursuits; I do know that I have always enjoyed math but have never thought seriously of becoming a mathematician.

Other students have also treated me differently than they have treated male students. Many male classmates have viewed me as a sex object or a romantic possibility instead of the intellectual counterpart I wish to be. Other females have often viewed me with suspicion or as competition, especially in drama classes where physical attractiveness and sex appeal can have much to do with success. I do feel that I fit in with the many other women on campus. However, it is sometimes difficult to function in a hierarchical system dominated by male thought patterns. I was well prepared for the experience, however, as I was encouraged in primary and secondary schools to be "good," that is to say, "studious and conforming." I was not expected to act out and rebel as the boys often were.

As a white student, my life has been much easier than the lives of students of other races. I am readily accepted by instructors and other students and am familiar with the customs and thought patterns of the white culture. People of my race are so well represented in course material that it tends to give us an inflated sense of self importance. Being white, however, has caused me other problems because I cannot understand what it is like to be of another race. I thought of myself as rather liberal and nonracist until I attended an on-campus rally for the rights of African-American students. I attended believing that the organizers would be pleased to see white supporters. Instead, the message to us was "The only way you can help is to fight racism by working among *your own* people. We do not want you working with us." This experience cast me into a cycle of questioning which may continue for the rest of my life. What is it like to be black in this society? In what ways are we different? In what ways are we alike? How much racism have I absorbed unconsciously, and how can I purge myself of it? To what degree am I responsible for my ancestors' possible transgressions?

As a practicing Wiccan, I am in a definite minority. Christian propaganda floods the campus and I have often had people try to convert me. I was raised without any particular religious dogma, but with the idea that Divinity equals Love equals the Universe equals everything: me and all that surrounds me. I was taught that limitless spiritual power resides inside me and that I could tap into it whenever I set my heart to it. From this base, I grew to embrace the nature religion/ magical craft that is Wicca. It is difficult at times, however, to function as a pagan in a world where everyone is assumed to be Judeo-Christian. If pre-monotheistic religions are reflected in course material at all, they are usually presented as silly superstition. I have never heard mentioned in class that there is anyone currently practicing such a religion. My lack of familiarity with the Bible sometimes hinders me when it is assumed to be common knowledge, but I hesitate to speak up and reveal my ignorance. In fact, I do not as a rule reveal my pagan practices unless I am rather certain I am speaking to an open-minded person. Persecution of witches still occurs today! My religious background does give me a certain edge, however. I believe that I am more open to nontraditional and cross-cultural views than are those who believe it is wrong to question their childhood beliefs. I have been drawn to a World Religions class and a Medieval World humanities class as well as to various churches and discussion groups in an attempt to understand the institutional Christianity which unavoidably affects my life.

Growing up in the middle class prepared me very well for university life. There was a strong emphasis on academics, and it was always assumed I would attend college. Neither shabbily poor nor snobbily rich, I have been readily accepted by students and faculty alike. Course material is centered on those of my class and, like my race, this social standing has trained me in the structure of the white male system; my family was neither too poor to fit in nor rich enough to escape it. I had long been curious as to what it might be like to be poor. A few years with little money and some food stamps helped me to get a glimpse of the less-privileged life. I lived it enough to realize that it is difficult to think beyond the next meal when the cabinets are bare. I have also wondered what it would be like to be well off, but of course Americans (through the media) are encouraged to dream of riches and are fed plenty of information on wealthy people. We, the people, are easier to control if our aspirations are centered on material wealth.

As a white, Wiccan, middle-class woman, the academic world has been welcoming yet alienating, comforting yet cold. As I make my way through this white male upper/middle class Christian-oriented maze, I constantly face new challenges in thought, language, attitudes, and assumptions.

—Cynthia

Lumps in the Melting Pot

The setting of a large university is quite unique. It is one of the few places where people of all races, nationalities, religions, and social classes share a common goal—the pursuit and attainment of knowledge. On a large scale, this diversity enhances the university community, but at the same time, it can be detrimental to certain individuals. Differences in race, age, and gender can make the university environment less appealing or even threatening to some students.

When I say that race can affect a student's liking of and success in the university, I am not referring to blatant racism. I have yet to hear the word *nigger* in a class or see a Ku Klux Klan T-shirt on campus. The race discrimination I am talking about is much more subtle. A perfect example can be found in the university orientation class that I am taking this semester. The instructor is an older white woman. She has no problem remembering or pronouncing the names of the white students, but at least half of the black students are never called on. This is because, unless they have names like John or Jane, she can't say them. The class has been in session for two months, and she has had plenty of time to familiarize herself with difficult names. I honestly question how comfortable a student can feel in a class where the instructor cannot call her by name at midsemester.

Age differences are also a cause of subtle discrimination at the university. This is evident only in my night class, a psychology course. One night, I was assigned to a paired discussion with a woman whom I would guess is fifty years old. She completely dominated the conversation with examples of her children, grandchildren, and yes, even her pets. I could not get a word in edgewise. She assumed that because she had a good thirty years on me, I didn't know anything. While I realize that experience is a great teacher, I am making an A in the class and could have contributed something to the discussion. Age discrimination can also work the other way. For example, there is a middle-aged woman in my Spanish class who seems very insecure about her work and the whole idea of being back in school. While she is no bilingual whiz, she knows just as much as everyone else in the class. Unfortunately, she is always nervous and has even made several jokes about "being too old for this."

Sex discrimination in the educational system seems to come more in the form of intimidation than actual harassment. I cannot really comment on the professors at ODU, because my high school experiences with male teachers were so bad that I purposefully registered for classes with female instructors only. My high school history teacher, for example, was so intimidating that nothing could be discussed. He was always right, and anyone who dared to question his opinion was treated to either a detention threat or "the look of death." I don't mean that this happened when students talked back; it happened when someone merely questioned a disputable fact. My tenth-grade driver's education teacher was a great intimidator, too. He used a different approach—rude jokes and comments about women. Needless to say, I am deathly afraid of registering for next semester, since I may have to have a male professor.

A large university environment is, in many ways, similar to the great American melting-pot concept. Over time, the mixture becomes smoother, but there are still some lumps. These lumps are qualities such as race, age, and gender that can set people apart. Because these differences are still so obvious and such great sources of discrimination, one must wonder if this mixture we are melting will ever be blended enough for everyone to enjoy.

—T. S. M.

Pushed to Go That Extra Mile

As an only child growing up with both parents until age five, I was always pushed to go that extra mile. My parents always made me work much harder at whatever I was doing than did the parents of my friends or relatives who were my age. I was also taught that you never stop in the middle of something; you always follow it through. After my parents' divorce, my mother expended all her extra energies to submerge me in school books. I honestly feel that she was harder on me because I was an African-American female growing up in the inner city. My mother always said that she wanted better for me than what she had. I really believe that this is why she was so hard on me.

My mother is by no means a rich woman. She is what most people consider middle- to upper-middle class. I feel that has had a lot to do with my feelings on education because I had to watch her struggle—working two or three jobs just to make things better. I have always been taught to accept who I am, and that money doesn't make the person. Even if we had been "filthy rich," that would not have made me a better person. It might have made things less complicated, but I probably wouldn't feel the way I do now toward life, and especially toward education.

As an African American at Old Dominion University, I sometimes feel that the academic program is not intended for me or others like me. I transferred to Old Dominion from Lincoln University, a historically black institution in Pennsylvania. I had chosen to attend a historically black college because twelve years of my academic life were spent at a private school where black history was only spoken of in February. I felt I needed a change of atmosphere. This private school had a population of about 40 percent African Americans, and I lived in an integrated area of the city, but I still felt I needed to explore my horizons and learn more about my culture. I transferred from Lincoln to this school because it was rumored that my department of concentration was going to lose its accreditation. I feel that the atmosphere here at Old Dominion is very different from Lincoln.

I observe people every day, and it's not a matter of fitting in because I have always been very self confident. I know how to make friends. It's just that here, the students, both black and white, seem so snobbish! I try not to think of it as having to do with certain social classes, but in most cases, that is just the reality of the matter. There are others (mostly females) who, when not in a group, admit that their families are not well off; however, when they get around other people, they feel they have to be phony and put on airs.

I have always had teachers who have asked why I am not very vocal in class. Apparently, they felt that I was an intelligent student who had something to offer. I rarely speak in class unless I have a question or something that I feel is important to say. This is true even in my education classes, where females are the majority. I am not shy, bashful, or embarrassed to speak, but unless something hits a nerve or I don't understand, I stay quiet. Some things that get me to talk are prejudicial statements, criticism of people who are less fortunate, and racial remarks. When issues such as these are brought up in class, I usually go on and on. My attitude is slightly different in every class depending upon how the class is organized and the overall attitudes of the teacher and the students. Once I am out of the classroom setting, I become more social.

I have come to college to prepare myself to teach. This career is and always has been female-dominated. Many families expect their little girls to become "schoolmarms." Not mine. When I entered college, I was a history major with a minor in political science and international studies. I wanted to go to law school, become a corporate lawyer, and then bring my experiences back to the classroom and teach. I can honestly say that no one deterred me from my original dreams but me. In high school, I began tutoring the homeless; at Lincoln I tutored, and here I am part of the Literacy Program. I simply have a love for helping others and sharing with them the knowledge that I have obtained.

I believe in my heart that being an African-American female in America is a struggle in itself. Going to college, whether historically black or otherwise, does not change this fact. Women in general still are not considered equal, but African-American females have it worse. Many people have placed stereotypical limits on what an African-American woman is capable of doing. I feel that this is an extremely hard thing to overcome. I know what I am capable of, and I refuse to let anyone change my mind.

At Old Dominion University, a school in the South, I have learned to deal with racism and other things that were never part of my education before. When I came here, I experienced for the first time being called a "black nigger." At my other university, where African Americans were the majority, I never had that problem, nor did I have that problem in high school. I do realize that I cannot let this deter me from my education, and I have no intention of letting that happen.

—Cherisse R. Echols

2

Belonging and Alienation in the Classroom

≥●

Introduction

One of the questions we posed to the student essayists was: "Do you feel as though you belong at ODU?" Our assumption, based on the literature of multiculturalism, was that those who felt at home at ODU would do better as students. How, then, does an increasingly diverse institution make all its students feel welcome?

Each individual embodies a unique and complex configuration of race, class, gender, age, sexual orientation, ethnicity, and religion. Cultural assumptions and stereotypes regarding these aspects of identity strongly influence whether a student feels like an outsider or a valued member of the university community. Students appear to have greater self-consciousness about feelings of alienation than about belonging, and because individuals whose identities place them outside the dominant groups often come to Old Dominion already well-schooled in marginality, there is an overrepresentation of minority students in this section.

Those persons who consider themselves part of the mainstream of society seem to derive a sense of belonging from their association with the dominant race, class, gender, and/or sexual orientation. Thus, they may take for granted their position of comfort within the academic community, not giving any thought to the "fit" between them and the institution. At the same time, some of these students also express painfully acquired feelings of ambivalence toward their secure status in the classroom. One author writes of her fear of being "politically incorrect," and another writer, a white male, describes his discomfort with being part of a group which may have oppressed others in the past.

Several white essayists of both sexes express deep anger and feelings of alienation because they believe they have been victimized by affirmative-action policies. These students resent the promotion of multiculturalism within the university; they are unwilling "to take a class on African Americans or Chinese Americans or Purple Polka Dot Americans." They state that such classes either hold no interest for them or unfairly "single out some minorities and not others."

The essays in this chapter suggest that in order to feel at home in the university classroom, individuals need to see some aspects of their own cultural identity reflected in the curriculum. Several writers vividly describe the individual and institutional attitudes that still serve as barriers for many minority students. One essayist asserts that an understanding of cultural diversity and an attitude of respect for each individual on the part of the instructor or advisor is necessary in order for each student to learn at peak capacity or to make his or her unique contribution to the class. In contrast, another essay shows how entrenched the idea of marginalized individuals *separating themselves* from the mainstream is among members of the dominant cultural groups. Its writer refers to America as a supposedly "classless society," assuming that a "level playing field" exists, that the accomplishments of individuals are determined solely by their own ability and hard work, and that marginalized persons have *chosen* to alienate themselves from the cultural mainstream. No minority students make this point.

Students who feel marginalized because of their race, gender, class, sexual orientation, or some other facet of their identity, employ many different coping strategies to increase their sense of belonging. Frequently, students who feel isolated from the university community at large are able to find a comfortable niche within extracurricular organizations composed of other individuals of the same race, sexual orientation, or political views. A gay man tells how he found support and eventually achieved a position of leadership in the Gay and Lesbian Student Union at ODU. A black woman concludes that her middle-class identity helps to compensate for the marginalization imposed by her race and gender. An African-American male derives a sense of belonging, of "insider" status, from his campus jobs. Students who have immigrated to the United States from other countries may seek to be assimilated by emulating the speech, dress, and manners of the mainstream.

On the other hand, the world view of several student authors enables them to resist the assimilation process and to take pride in their uniqueness and heritage. A black Muslim woman, for example, asserts that it is she who "give[s] the college shape and meaning by attending." Another African-American woman relates to the "lost generations" of her enslaved and oppressed ancestors and, despite her feelings of alienation, achieves a sense of self-satisfaction by succeeding academically against the odds.

Most of the student essayists in this chapter—survivors of the institution—have managed, through a wide variety of coping mechanisms, to deal with the obstacles they encountered as a function of their cultural differences. These students have achieved some sense of belonging at Old Dominion University.

૨૧

Nothing Reflects Me at this University

My academic career has been a phenomenal growth experience. When I ponder my place in Old Dominion University, I do not feel I have one. However, this feeling is not confined to the university. As an African American, I often finish a semester having had only six to eight other African Americans in all of my classes. As a woman, I finish many semesters having had a majority of males in my class. It is most disturbing to read the school newspaper and find nothing reflecting African-American females at this university. To further complicate matters, I am a lesbian.

While I was a senior in high school, I went around visiting different schools. I was looking for a place where I could detect the presence of other African Americans and/or homosexuals and signs of the chance that an African-American woman could be respected and appreciated. Not one historically white school in Virginia that I visited seemed to welcome anyone but white males.

I feel that some subjects were not as available for me to study as others. I vividly recall my freshman advisor. He did not take my freshman schedule as seriously as he took that of other students in the group session during orientation. I interpreted the slight as a reflection of his assumption that I was not likely to be around come senior year. Therefore, why should he waste his time? When I finally pressed him for guidance, he suggested I take less-challenging classes than he had suggested for anyone else. In my opinion, that was a deliberate insult. As it was a group session, we did not have our academic records with us, and I know there is no way he could have memorized all of our transcripts. I can therefore infer that some observable characteristic of mine made him treat me differently. I am undoubtedly not the first one he has treated this way, nor will I be the last. Perhaps the last four years have made me cynical (yes, I made it through four years), but I think he is representative of a vast majority of his colleagues. I was fortunate enough to escape him as an instructor, but if I hadn't, would my grade have reflected his biases? I can assure you that has been the case with many other students.

In order to be an effective conveyor of information, a teacher has to create a safe atmosphere for learning. A professor needs to understand and respect those whom he is trying to teach. It is necessary for students to feel that they belong to and are a part of the class. Each student must feel as valued as every other student, or interaction will be limited and learning will suffer. I am puzzled by professors and educators who attempt to teach people of whom they have no knowledge. How practical is that? How can you teach someone that you don't know? This argument holds in early childhood education, too, and that is the reason future teachers have to be taught how to understand the young people they will be responsible for teaching.

—Theresa Scott

If I Had Not Been a White Male

I am a white, middle-class male, and have been a student at Old Dominion University for the past two and a half years. Since I have been a student, I cannot recall a time in which I ever felt that I was discriminated against because of my class, gender, or race. There have been times that I have felt outnumbered in a classroom, mainly because of the field I have chosen. I am a middle-school education major, and as a male, I am a minority in the field.

Sometimes, I decide to voice my opinion in a classroom discussion. The females in my class occasionally turn and look at me and sometimes gang up on me because they don't like what I have to say. I have my opinion and they have theirs, and so I stand my ground and hold tight to my opinion. Sometimes these situations begin to get out of hand, and some male bashing starts to happen; usually my professor steps in to get things back under control. This is not a common scenario in the classes I have been in, but it has occurred. When something like this happens to me, it tends to make me think twice before voicing my opinion again. I don't like feeling that way, but I am not one who likes to sit and argue when I know nothing will get resolved.

Once, in a diagnostic reading class, the professor repeatedly described as black and female a remedial reading student who used nonstandard English. This was an awkward situation for me because I knew that what the professor was saying would have irritated me if I had not been a white male. If I looked at the comments from the point of view of a black female, I could see how they might have sounded offensive. From my perspective, though, the comments were meant to reinforce a lecture point, not to degrade someone because of their race or gender.

There have been specific subjects such as science and social studies which I have been drawn towards because of my background. There were also courses which I have tried to avoid. Last semester, I took an upper-level class in African-American politics that I never would have taken if it had not been required to complete my major. I went into the class very skeptical and unsure of what to expect. At first, I was totally turned off by the subject and the material because I had no background in them. Now that I have completed this class, I look back on it and realize not only how much I struggled to get through it but also how much I learned and gained from the experience. I now look at Malcolm X and Martin Luther King, Jr., the Black Panther Party, and the civil rights movement in a totally different way. This class really opened my eyes to historical figures and political situations that I knew nothing about, and I have benefited greatly.

—Todd Woodall

At Ease Only When Alone

I am an African American whose parents sent him to white schools, some of them in another state, to make sure I received a solid education. Having been ridiculed and made the butt of jokes for being the only black in a class of whites, and not having been raised to identify with other African Americans in an everyday setting, I find myself completely at ease only when alone. My family (my father in particular) grew up at a time when there were little or no opportunities for blacks, and they were determined that I have the skills and possess the thought processes to take full advantage of, or even create, openings to get ahead. At a very young age I was taught to read phonetically, instilled with the value of logic, and instructed to speak without slang in a clear and concise manner. The discussion of opinions in my family was limited to "Yes, Dad. I couldn't agree with you more." Anything less was, and is, met with contempt or an air of patronizing an obvious idiot.

Coming from a family of very open civil-rights advocates, I have been taught since birth that there was nothing that should be closed to me, that the only limit to what I could do was the limit of what I could think of doing. One particular course, however, in which I felt ill at ease was a U.S. history class in which the instructor had done his dissertation on the premise that slaves had good lives while in captivity and that the bulk of them did not want to leave their masters. This position would have been a tolerable one if he had allowed room for dissent, but instead he regarded his opinion as indisputable fact.

The way I am treated by instructors and fellow students is primarily a result of what I project, and what I don't, although I do feel that there is a tendency to assume that I'm just trying to slide by. Speaking up and making intelligent comments on the subject matter seem to mark me as a superior student. Coming from a nonminority student, I think these behaviors would be considered nothing special. I feel as though anyone who doesn't fit into the carefully crafted construct of blacks set forth by the media (lazy, unintelligent, looking for a handout) is somehow considered an extraordinary case to be admired. In my classes and study groups, I feel as though I am a representative of the African-American male. How teachers and other students perceive me will affect what they think when they see other young black men walking down the street.

—Jacob

I Call Myself an American

I do not feel that I am treated any differently than others at ODU because I am a twenty-three-year-old white, low-income, Protestant, heterosexual male. Each person brings his own set of life experiences to class. I think of myself as being the type of person who will try to get along with anyone. I come from a family of very intelligent people, some of whom are writers. I also come from a family of readers. I, however, dislike to read or write; I prefer to learn from discussion. I'm a good student, and I learn a lot in a class that debates topics— rather than one in which the usual assignment is to read chapter three and write an essay.

If I'm having trouble in a class, it would be easy to say that the teacher doesn't like me because I'm white and he's black. That's something I might have done in junior high. If I'm treated differently from others in class, it is more than likely because of something I've said; I'm outspoken as well as out-going. The problem probably has nothing to do with my gender or sexual preference.

I would, however, feel strange in a Black history class. It doesn't interest me; neither does Irish history or Japanese history. I believe in not separating myself from others. It is simply my right not to have an interest in those subjects. My personality draws me to study certain subjects, not my race, sex, class (I thought America was supposed to be a classless society), or age.

If anyone thinks he is being discriminated against, for any reason, he should ask himself two questions: How do I see myself? Do I try to separate myself from others? Some people separate *themselves* from others and then complain that others separate themselves from *them*. African Americans, for example, separate themselves from other Americans by not calling themselves Americans. I have no desire to be referred to as an English, German (Jewish), Irish, Scottish, French, Native-American American, although that would be correct. I'm proud of my heritage. *I* am an American. *We* are Americans.

I'm not saying that there is not discrimination; there is. I am saying that separating ourselves because of age, race, nationality, social or income class, or gender is not the answer. In my classes, the students and the professors practice being politically correct. Racial issues are shoved down my throat every day, especially by the media. That's why I've pounced on racial issues. It seems that every time an African American has a problem of almost any kind, the media calls it a racial issue.

—D. W. Red

My Money Is as Good as Anybody Else's

At a very early age, I became aware of various limitations that people would place upon me simply because I was black. I attended a predominantly white high school, and I noticed that many of the teachers assumed that my college choices were limited to only black universities. I decided that my race should not be an issue in choosing a college; therefore, I took it upon myself to choose an institution that would best suit my academic needs and not just my racial needs. When I chose Old Dominion as my college, I prepared myself for handling situations which black students have to deal with while attending a predominantly white university. Although times have changed since the blatant racial discrimination of earlier years, we still live in a world where "white is right," and some people will never be able to see past the color of my skin.

I have been told by many people that I was born with two disabilities: first that I am black, and second that I am a woman. I have refused to let myself be discouraged by others' ignorance. There are professors and students at this university who would like nothing better than to see me fail. I have had professors discourage my future plans, and students who refuse to acknowledge my presence and my ideas. There are often times when I feel as though black perspectives and female perspectives are not part of course material. Sometimes, it is difficult to get myself to share my ideas in class for fear that they will be rejected by the majority of students who do not share my experiences and do not understand them. In relation to my race and gender and its effect on my participation, I have noticed that I am less likely to voice my opinion on black/white issues than I am to voice my opinion on male/female related issues. This is probably because there is usually more of a support system for me on male/female debates simply because there are more females in the class. When I am speaking on a black/white issue, there are usually only one or two other blacks who can empathize with the position I am taking.

My social class has an impact on my role as a student; although it plays a smaller part than race and gender, it is still an important component. Coming from a middle-class background, I was more prepared for university life. I realized that, in order to function and succeed in this world, I would have to be able to understand how to work with more than just black people. My middle-class values seem to be in accordance with many of the professors and students at this university, so that has not offered a big disturbance in participating in class discussion.

There will always be those people who make it their business to make sure that I know that I am not welcomed and do not belong at this university. But it is my philosophy that my money is as good as anybody else's, and as long as I can afford to go here, then I belong. I belong here for the simple fact that it is my choice, I make good grades, and I am secure in my future plans while attending this university. There are definitely aspects of my identity which enhance my sense of belonging. For example, my religion tells me that I am no different from anyone else and that I should not have to be subjected to the judgment of others.

It is very important for everyone to take a step back and try to see a situation from the viewpoint of another. I am forced to take that step every day of my life in order to function in a predominantly white university. I believe that it is time for others to try and see where I am coming from, and then they may be better able to understand my struggle.

—Tonya Anderson

A Dream Deferred

He was buried in his cap and gown, clutching the diploma that was to have been his in less than two weeks as he was lowered into the gray earth that replaced the future he would never experience. There would be no college or career or family for the friend I had known since elementary school. Earlier in the year, he had been near me at the homecoming game when another teenager was shot in the stomach. Unlike my friend, that boy's future remains full of possibilities; his life did not escape through six bullet wounds to the head. A few days after that incident at the game, blood was spilled again during a routine morning at school. This time it splattered on the floor and stained the concrete sidewalk by the bus ramp as a boy ran from the drug dealer who threw him through a trophy case after a deal went bad. Later his face was a spider web of deep, purple scars. I could still see the surrounding holes through which the doctors had sewn black thread to hold his once-handsome face together. I averted my eyes at this, as well as at the gang colors, black eyes, and bruised knuckles that pervaded my daily life from nine to three o'clock, because I did not want to acknowledge that these pictures were a part of my life. This was my high school, and I wanted to get as far away from it as possible. The violence, racism, and inequality there shaped me—not by showing me how to be, but by demonstrating what kind of person I would struggle not to become. I did not endeavor to be me; rather I endeavored not to be them. I still have resentment for those who made my high school years unhappy, the circumstances of my life that have crushed my dreams, and the society that lets it all happen.

It was hard not to become prejudiced. I have always believed that people can give you so many other reasons not to like them that it is a cliché to dislike them simply because of their race. I am, and always will be, prejudiced against ignorant people. However, the bruises that covered my body when those ignorant people shoved me out of the way to get closer to the altercation of the day made me focus my prejudice on those who hurt me. They were predominately African-American males dressed in loud colors with language as brash as their demeanor. Though hardly comprising the entire population of black males at my school, they were the so-called "bad apples that ruined the bunch." Every muscle of my being tenses when I walk by such a rowdy group. Conditioning has told me to beware, even though I feel like a horrible person when I think about how I do not know any of them. In high school I avoided the "average" classes that never got anything accomplished because "they" were in them, and no teacher or student was safe from the remarks they made. I numbed my over-emotional spirit and feigned deafness when I walked by their groups in the hall, pretending not to hear, "Hey, bitch! Wanna piece of this nigger? Whatsa matta? You prejudiced or somethin'?" Shaking, I hurried down the hall wondering if I was and if they had made me that way. They made me excel in school because I did not want to be in classes with them; I did not want to live near them; I did not want them to steal my future as they had stolen my friend's. I hoped to go away to college and start over. But more unfortunate circumstances prevented that.

I became resentful of many of my friends when their dreams came true at what I perceived to be the expense of my own. Why did the "system," in awarding scholarships, take ball-handling capabilities, race, and family background into account over intelligence, potential, and merit? I hate being jealous of my friends, but I was a valedictorian who worked very hard for the achievement of a very high grade point average. I wanted to go to Pepperdine University and become an esteemed journalist, but lack of money prevented it. I found myself losing scholarships to minority students with lower GPA's, SAT's, and less well-rounded extracurricular activities than I. My bitterness over this caused me to lose a good friend. Her 3.0 GPA and dark skin beat my 4.4 and pale complexion for an academic scholarship for which I had also applied. A rude "Who cares?" escaped my lips when she told me about her accomplishment. Although I apologized many times and explained why I had said it, she never forgave me and to this day will go to any measure to pretend that I no longer walk the face of this earth. When I watched my dear friend Chris sign a four-year contract for a full athletic scholarship to Penn State, I had to excuse myself to go to the bathroom where I wept, having found out the night before that my partial academic scholarship would not be enough for me to attend Pepperdine. I even began to resent my sister, who had the nerve to be born first and to require my parents' help to pay for four years at the University of Virginia. She was at a school she liked, while I was having an emotional breakdown at the prospect of remaining near what I so longed to escape.

I often sit in class at Old Dominion and ponder such abstractions as "Why me?" I joined the Honors Program, following my instincts that there I would not be surrounded by people I fear and people I feel are not very intelligent. I like it, but I do not like that I like it. I feel I deserve more than a school that Barron's rates in the middle on its scale of America's colleges. I have not found anyone at ODU to dislike, but I dislike the school because I did not want to end up here. My old fears are dissipating, and new ones are taking their place. Fearing hallways less, I now fear being politically incorrect and admitting how I view things due to the violence and discrimination I have seen. I avoid voicing such opinions for fear of offending someone. Although I frequently join in class discussions, I will avoid or screen any comments on the issues of race and the "system." I will not take a class such as sociology that I fear will often delve into this discourse. I will not take a class on African Americans or Chinese Americans or Purple Polka Dot Americans because I do not think that it is healthy to single out some minorities and not others. The system of scholarships in America does this, and in no way has it ever benefited me. I have never seen a class on "Dutch American Studies," nor did I learn of any scholarships for Dutch Americans. I have learned a lesson that wise parents try to teach: "Hey, kid, life's not fair." Am I bitter? Possibly. Am I angry? Definitely.

Langston Hughes asks, "What happens to a dream deferred?" But his possible answers do not include my own. Unattained dreams make us search for new possibilities in our circumstances. But we never forget that our dreams escaped us. The conditions under which our dreams dwindled and eventually disappeared remain, and often the dark feelings they cause are hard to suppress. I will never be content with ODU, though I find myself liking it more and more. As this happens, I consider abandoning my plans to transfer to a different college. I imagine I fit in quite nicely with the Honors Program at a college near downtown Norfolk's violent streets. After all, I gave my valedictory speech to a sullen class, a class smaller by one whose obituary had appeared in the paper less than two weeks before.

—M. K. B.

Outside the Mainstream of Society

In kindergarten and first grade, no one would have expected me to ever do well in school. I often cried to go back home to be with my mother. My teacher wanted to keep me in kindergarten another year because I couldn't tie my shoes, and in first grade, I was put in a special section to help me learn to read. However, by the time I was in fifth grade, I had progressed to the most advanced reading section in my class.

In eleventh and twelfth grade, I continued to do well in school. I graduated from high school in the top ten percent of my class. Until this point, I was a member of the racial and gender majority. My family lived in a rural area and there were very few, if any, African Americans in the schools I attended. My parents, teachers, and guidance counselor encouraged me to set career goals, do well in school, and to go to college.

While growing up, I was taught such values as idealism, love, fairness, patience, loyalty, and responsibility by my parents, church, and television heroes. I also knew what it was like to fall outside the mainstream of society. My family were Seventh-Day Adventists who went to church on Saturday instead of Sunday, and I have been a vegetarian since eighth grade. I also realized that I was attracted to members of my own sex from the time I hit puberty in seventh grade, although I did not acknowledge to myself that I was gay until around eleventh grade. I was afraid of how people would react, so I hid this part of myself in high school. I only suffered slight teasing from people who thought that I might be gay.

After high school, I looked for a college that offered a degree in electrical engineering. I had originally wanted to go to a school in Georgia near an uncle of mine who is also gay. I thought that if I went there, he could help me to meet other gay people. My plans to go to college in Georgia fell through because I could get free tuition if I went to college in Virginia. My dad is a Vietnam veteran on 100 percent disability. I could only find three colleges in Virginia that offered a four-year degree in electrical engineering: Virginia Tech, Norfolk State, and Old Dominion University. I didn't want to go to Virginia Tech because I thought I would have better luck meeting other gay people if I were in a larger city. I decided against Norfolk State because I thought I would feel uncomfortable and out of place as a white student. I finally decided to go to ODU.

During my orientation, I felt reassured that I had made the right choice. The student newspaper had some letters to the editor written about gay issues, and the student handbook mentioned a phone number to call about gays and lesbians on campus. During my first semester, I went to my first gay and lesbian support group meeting. I also began attending the newly formed Gay and Lesbian Student Union and a gay and lesbian youth group in the area.

During the spring semester of my second year, my partner of almost a year broke up with me. I dropped most of my classes by the end of the semester, and the Veterans' Administration wanted their money back. All these things led me to drop out of ODU for a semester and to change my major to sociology.

When I came back to ODU, I became president of the Gay and Lesbian Student Union, a position I would hold for the next year and a half. Although I am a strong introvert, I have become very outgoing and visible on lesbian and gay issues at ODU. I am one of a few people involved in getting the university administration to address lesbian and gay issues following the antigay graffiti on campus in 1992. I believe that the invisibility of gays and lesbians fosters stereotypes, myths, and other misconceptions about homosexuality and deprives those struggling with their sexual orientation of positive role models. As a result of my openness, I have been harassed by other students. I once found a group of people standing across the parking lot from my car with what appeared to be a stick or a bat. I feel lucky that a friend gave me a ride to the door of my car that night. I later found key scratches in the paint of my car. I also often hear people in my classes talking about "fags" and "queers." I usually don't say anything because I don't really like conflict. Since I don't know how people in my classes will react to my sexual orientation, I am usually somewhat disconnected from them.

I have enjoyed my sociology courses, and I have been making much better grades than I did in engineering. I have been particularly interested in discussions on minorities, stereotypes, inequality, and oppression, since being gay puts me in a socially oppressed group. I find myself sympathetic to members of other oppressed groups, and I am interested in the similarities and differences which exist in the different forms of oppression. My current career goal is to work for social change for gays, lesbians, and bisexuals, but I also feel committed to fight other oppressions as well.

In the courses I have taken, issues regarding homosexuality are usually only briefly mentioned, and sometimes not at all. I think this is sad because of the general ignorance in society on these issues and the continued prejudice and oppression resulting from this ignorance.

As a white male with excellent grades in high school, I was encouraged to do well and no limits were placed on me. My sexual orientation had little affect on my education until I went to college. In college, being gay has made a major impact on my choice of study, my career goals, my reactions, and the way people treat me in the classroom.

—Melvin Frizzell

I Do Not Feel Like an Outsider

I am a quadriplegic student at Old Dominion University. I maneuver around campus in a motorized wheelchair. The campus is accessible for the most part, but there are a few exceptions. The building in which most of my classes are located has two problems with its design. The most problematic are the elevators: there are only three small ones for a nine-story building. They are slow, at best, and often one or two of them are not even working. During my first semester at the university, I was late to my anthropology class several times and did not go to see professors in their offices because of the elevator situation. The other problem with the building is the layout of the ground floor. To get to the elevators, I must enter one set of doors, but in order to get to the classrooms on the ground floor, I must enter another set of doors because of a small set of stairs between the elevators and the classrooms. So, after I finish my class on the second floor, I must take the elevator to the first floor, leave the building, go halfway around it, and enter the second set of doors to get to my next class. This is not a problem on days when the weather is nice, but on rainy or cold days it is. My developmental psychology class was on the second floor of another building, but on the second day of class, the elevator broke and I could not get to my class. Luckily, my professor was able to move the class to the first floor, but if it had been a laboratory class, I would not have been so lucky because such classes cannot be moved.

Overall though, my first year on the Old Dominion campus has been a pleasant experience. The university has an Office of Disability Services. Its staff met with me before I entered the university setting and helped me know what to expect. They also prepared a letter for me to give to my professors so they would be aware of any adaptations I would need for the classes. The only adaptations I require are the taking of tests at the Office of Disability Services with a scribe and the use of a note taker in class. All my professors have been wonderful. For example, my English composition professor allowed me to leave the classroom and go wherever I felt comfortable to write my in-class essays because of my need to speak to my note taker; my anthropology professor was understanding of my being late for class because of the problem with the elevators; and my judicial process and behavior professor permitted me to take my exams home so that I could take them at my convenience.

Being a disabled student at the university does not make me feel like an outsider. My fellow students and professors do not treat me differently from anyone else. For example, I am included in class discussions as much as everyone else, and my philosophy professor asked me to read a paper at an Academic Honors Association meeting. No one gives me special treatment, and my professors have the same expectations of me as of my classmates. I think everyone brings their own unique identity, based on race, gender, disability or whatever, into the classroom. Any facet of that identity should add to the classroom experience and not hinder any student.

—Jennifer Budy

Americanized

I came to this country in 1982 when I was twelve years old. I am an Asian Indian by birth and, needless to say, I experienced a major culture shock when I immigrated to the United States.

Everything I did or said seemed to distinguish me from my classmates, and I don't mean in a flattering way. Gradually, I learned how to act, how to dress, and even how to talk. My Indian accent was thick and heavy. I don't have a trace of it now, and I don't think I can even imitate an Indian accent anymore. Do I feel ashamed that I seem to have lost touch with my heritage? Sure. I do some soul searching every now and then, but I like who I am right now. I may appear different on the outside, but I still have the same values and traits that make me who I am. I have managed to adjust remarkably well; I don't think you will find many Asians more "Americanized" than I am.

My first experience in an American school took place when I was a seventh grader. I found the classes relatively easy, especially in mathematics and English. However, I found there was a great difference in the way the classes were conducted compared to my classroom experiences in India. Students there never had much in-class interaction with other students or with the teacher. Usually, the teacher would walk in and lecture for most of the class period and then use the last few minutes to answer any questions. Here in the States, students communicate during class and express their views a lot more. The only time I spoke aloud in class was when I was called on to answer a question. So I wasn't used to how often American students verbalized in class. I was so intimidated by how well they were able to express their views that I became a silent student, even though I knew a lot of the answers to the teacher's questions. I would only speak aloud in class when I was called upon to do so.

Over a period of approximately ten years, I began to slowly emerge from my shell. Maybe one of the reasons I was so afraid to speak up in class was because of my thick accent, and I didn't want to feel any more distant from my classmates than I already did. As I slowly lost my accent and became more "Americanized" in other ways, I began to feel more confident. I am still one of the silent students in class; I communicate better in smaller groups than I do in larger ones. My strong points are definitely reading and writing. I have my parents to thank for that since I was encouraged to read from a very early age. Most of my friends were also avid readers; we would often discuss different books and even exchange books with each other. I know this wouldn't have occurred if I had been born in the United States. There are too many distractions here with television and shopping malls. I have felt some of my reading and writing skills eroding in the time that I have been here. I don't read for fun anymore; the only reading I do is required reading for school. I just don't feel I want to devote time to pleasure reading anymore. The abundance of distractions in this country is the primary reason that many Americans have such atrocious writing skills. However, American kids also have exceptional verbal skills, something I wish I had developed better when I was a kid.

In terms of this university, I do feel comfortable here. In fact, I am happier here than I ever thought I would be. I've made a lot of friends in my dorm. I've also been to the beach every weekend, and I've managed to keep up with my studies. I don't feel like I have any real obstacles to overcome anymore, but that is probably because I have had a full decade to adjust to this culture. I still have problems when my instructors discuss the Bible because Christianity is not my religion, and I have a really hard time understanding certain references that my classmates seem to have no problem understanding. All things considered, though, I feel very lucky to be in this country and to have the opportunity to fully enjoy Western life. I love it!

—A. A.

My Entitlement and My Mission

My personal vision of life is so broad that it is hard to narrow it, especially in terms of gender, race, social class, and religion. I have come to understand that as human beings we all possess uniqueness that is blurred until we reach a level of understanding that is compatible with the oneness of creation. Questions based on social analysis are superficial and keep us from having a real meaning and purpose in life. I have chosen the religion of Al-Islam, so I am a Muslim, African-American, female, wife, and mother of five children and of humanity. This list contains categories that I have chosen and some that were ordained. It is not written in order of importance, but nevertheless gives the identity of the person writing this essay for those who need it.

I am on a mission, just like everyone else in creation, and the mission is a part of my entitlement. I hope and pray that my presence at Old Dominion University has had more of an impact on faculty, staff, and students than the college has had on me; that is the way it should be. I give the college shape and meaning by attending. My uniqueness as an individual should bring originality that will fit with the other pieces of creation that I come to witness, embrace, or reject but that will nevertheless have an effect on my being. It should not be a one-way street. I belong everywhere that my entitlement

chooses to take me. I do not feel uncomfortable in any classroom because of my individual choices which make me
unique. Nor do I feel inferior because of the ordained choices
that the Almighty creator (Allah) has chosen for me. I will get
looks from people, and they may not quite understand where
I am coming from or where I am trying to go, but that is all
right. My views on certain issues may not be the views of the
majority or the minority but that is all right, too.

My whole life is a learning experience and I feel open and
broad enough in actions and thoughts to think globally and
universally. The lessons that I have learned are evident all
around me in the bigger scheme of things, the creation. Flow-
ers, the animals, and the plants do not keep statistics on their
self-worth, nor do they compare themselves with one another
to determine which is greater or better. Who is allowed to keep
the record and define your status or self-worth and what contributions you can or can not make to humanity?

My experience for the remainder of this life will be what
I am entitled to. My entitlement because of gender, race, social
class, religion, nationality, age, sexual orientation, and physical
disabilities depends upon previous decisions of God. He then
blesses me to act upon them. My college education does not
define who or what I am. It is just a small part of my entitlement and my mission. I view myself as a free human being
with an entitlement that has been bestowed upon me. I will try
to use this entitlement, with all its richness and uniqueness, to
fulfill my mission as it relates to creation. Those who feel it
necessary to categorize me in defining "humanity" by defining
"who or what I am" will have missed the whole point of my
existence.

—Clarita Mujahid

I Carry the Lost Generations

We wear the mask that grins and lies,
It hides our cheeks and shades our eyes,—
This debt we pay to human guile;
With torn and bleeding hearts we smile,
And mouth with myriad subtleties.

—"We Wear the Mask," Paul Laurence Dunbar

I am a middle-class African-American woman, and I wear the mask. I wear the mask not out of guilt or shame but out of a constant need to protect myself from a world that does not appreciate my existence and patiently awaits my failure. When I walk into any classroom, I carry with me the hopes and dreams of lost generations of people who never got the chance to be free. I am the embodiment of three hundred years of shattered dreams and broken spirits. They were the nameless, faceless, voiceless generations of people who endured the agonies of ritual hatred and racism. Their undeniable courage and strength are the reason I am here. The spirit of God and the spirit of these lost generations are the sources of my academic success. I carry them with me wherever I go, and I strive to achieve in their honor.

I had never considered myself to be intelligent. So, in the beginning, I did not feel as if I belonged at this university. But that all changed after I earned my first college A. It was in English, my best subject, and an African-American male was my instructor. He openly expressed his expectations for his students at the outset of the course, and I worked very hard not to disappoint him. At that point, I realized that I belonged in college. I knew that this would be the place where I would not only receive a degree, but also I would discover my purpose in life. I must admit that at first I thought maybe the A was a one-time occurrence, but consistently an A emerges every semester. I have finally convinced myself that I am a good student and that I deserve the academic recognition that is bestowed upon me. I do not always speak out in class because I feel more comfortable in small groups. However, I am not afraid to let the world know that I am intelligent and that I understand what is going on around me. I am generally open to any topic of discussion and am always willing to hear other viewpoints.

I do not walk along this scholastic pathway alone. I carry with me the unfulfilled aspirations of those African Americans who dedicated their lives to secure my future. The debt I owe them can never be repaid. However, I have decided to be another shining example of the rewards gained from their tireless efforts to overcome oppression. They are a part of me, and I am a part of them. We share the same blood and the same tears—together we stand as one. We do not want to rule the world; we only want to feel as if we belong. We know that we have not completely overcome, but we acknowledge that we have positively progressed from whence we originated.

I dedicate my academic success to the countless slaves who never realized actual freedom, to the men and women of the civil rights movement who relentlessly protested in the name of equality, to Dr. Martin Luther King Jr. in memory of "the dream," to the teenagers who have lost their lives in the streets—who will never manifest their full potential, to Joy D. Spell whose life would have undoubtedly been another shining example if it had not ended in a tragic accident, and to my parents who have given me their endless love and support.

When I take that final walk across the stage to receive my degree, the lost generations will proudly walk with me. No one will be able to see them or hear them shout for joy, but I'll be aware of their presence and I'll share in the celebration. In that moment, they will face the world that rejected them, and they will smile. In that instant, they will finally know what it feels like to belong. They will know that, in spite of it all, their lives were not lost in vain, that the world gained something from their existence. My hopes are that I never lose their spirit, that my accomplishments always bring them honor, and that they are as eternally proud of me as I will always be of them.

—Michelle L. Wilson

The University Is My Second Home

I am the youngest of three children, and I will be the last child of the first generation in my family to graduate from college. My siblings chose practical majors which would further their career goals, and they have attained considerable success in those fields. For that same reason, I chose to major in geography with an emphasis in environmental studies. This was reputed to be one of the "hot" job fields for the nineties. Although it was not my first choice of study, I thought it might offer more of an opportunity financially than one of my true passions, such as history, philosophy, or political science. I have found that I am one of a handful of African Americans who have chosen this field of study here at ODU.

I look at the college classroom as a crucible in which knowledge is created. It is a place that cries out for students to bring their own unique ideas and experiences. These things should be encouraged in the quest for knowledge, understanding, truth, and justice. However, I have noted that with these varying ideas come preconceived notions, stereotypes, bigotry, and ignorance.

I have found that my race can have both positive and negative effects with regard to my identity within the classroom. As an African-American male, I believe that I am able to give better opinions with regard to the impact of racism and economic oppression on minorities than some of my peers, since they are only observers of certain situations of injustice and I have had actual experiences. I have also found instances where my race has been perceived as a negative with regard to opinions I might offer. For example, in one of my sociology classes, we were discussing integration versus segregation. I made the point that segregation and slavery have relegated African Americans in the past to second-class citizenship and even to this day have hampered our efforts to reach social and economic security as a race. My opinion was considered biased by some of my classmates, even though they had no practical experience with discrimination at all.

If one is a minority, one is stereotyped into political categories as well. It is a perception that most minority members are Democrats; I have noticed in class that if I happen to be in favor of some Republican legislation, many of my peers are astounded. Members of my own race seem to see me more as an individual than a stereotype. For minorities to succeed and elevate their quality of life, they must be willing to play both sides of the political arena in an effort to further their overall cause. I feel that this is true because if one's vote is always expected to be Democratic, that vote can easily be taken for granted. In that case, minorities can never truly achieve their own agenda through participation in only one party.

My age plays a significant role in the classroom as well. I have noticed that there exists a love/hate relationship between younger and older students. Older students tend to participate more in class, do somewhat better on tests, and apply what has been taught to practical experiences. I believe this is the case because older students are usually more focused since they have experienced more of life. This seems to alienate us from younger students. They either learn to take advantage of the wisdom of the older students or to despise them.

I have also had the honor and the privilege to work as a student assistant here on campus in several high-profile positions that have afforded me the opportunity to interact with faculty and staff on both a business and social level. Through this interaction, I have attained an almost "insider" status. When I enter the classroom, I do not lose my distinction of being a coworker, which to some degree sets me apart from my fellow students. There are times when my job and class schedules conflict. However, through the job identity I bring into the classroom, I can be allowed some latitude. ODU has become more than just the university I attend. In some respects, it has become a second home.

—D. H.

An "Other" in the Classroom

When I was in grade school years ago, we were given tests using scan sheets to "bubble in." We wrote our names in the boxes and filled in our student numbers and oddly, I thought, were required to indicate our race. For me, the choice was easy. I was not white. I was not black. I was "other." I didn't realize then that the scan sheet, like many of the textbooks, videos, and children's programs in the school, failed to recognize minority groups other than black Americans. In American society, Filipino Americans, Chinese and Korean Americans, Native Americans, and Mexican Americans were lumped together in one large, faceless category and labeled "other." Like shades of gray, we were nondistinct hues, formless and undefined in a world colored in black and white. But that didn't bother me then. I was never without friends of my race and had many white friends and black friends, as well. The question of "fitting in" was never pertinent.

When I began my university studies at Old Dominion in the fall of 1987, however, I no longer felt as much a part of "the group." Often, I was the only Asian student among dozens of white students in the class, my black hair a startling contrast to the sea of blonde and brown, my skin much darker than their tans. In large lecture rooms, at least one-fifth of the students were black, but there were not nearly as many minority students as there had been in my high school class. More than once, I overhead discussions in class about the Japanese "taking over the country." I heard people speak with anger about those "yellow bastards" with "Chinky eyes" and it made me cringe inside. Although I am Filipino, remarks such as those are offensive and humiliating to me, as are insults about any minority group.

During my third year at the university, I took my first accounting class. Here, I was a "double minority"; the female sex was "other." Male students outnumbered female students by at least two to one, and all my professors were men. For the first time, I felt unduly peculiar in a classroom setting. I couldn't help feeling inadequate because I wasn't as assertive as many of the male students in class about asking questions. Sometimes when people looked at me, I wondered if they thought that I shouldn't be there, but I held firm.

During my junior year, I made an appointment with my accounting advisor. He reviewed my course requirements and smiled as I asked him for the earliest registration date possible so that I could get the classes I needed for graduation. I left, and my friend, who is white, went in to make his appointment with the advisor. Later on that day, I discovered that the accounting advisor awarded my male friend, who was a year behind me in his studies, an earlier registration date than mine. I couldn't help feeling that I was a victim of either sexism, racism, or both.

I changed my major to elementary/middle-school education the following semester. I can't say that I did it solely because I didn't belong in the accounting field, but it was refreshing to be able to interact with more female students in all of my classes. I immediately felt more comfortable. I began to speak more freely and ask more questions in my classes. I even made the dean's list twice.

However, I am still a minority in the field of education. Last semester, I was one of only two Asians in my science methods class. But I am an optimist. I believe that someday this will change. Someday, Asians and other minorities will be more visible in the educational system, the accounting field, and all other disciplines. Someday, we will realize the beauty in diversity and learn to appreciate and respect what is different. Someday, we will see the people beneath the shades of gray.

—Mary S.

3

Making Sense of Our Lives Through Education

ह॒

Introduction

What students learn in the classroom provides some of them with the conceptual foundation they need to make the connection between their lived experience and what they study. Other individuals' life experiences guide them to a particular educational path. Often, both these processes occur.

Some of the students in this section speak of education as a liberating force in their lives, which enables them to both understand and redefine themselves. Many of them write of initial failures that eventually gave way to academic success and of how they found a way to make sense of their lives through their educational experience. This process of reconceptualization is facilitated by the complex interplay of students' individual life experiences, teachers' encouragement, relevant course material, and an educational climate that welcomes diversity. Such an educational environment enables students to expand their vision of their own potential and life goals as it challenges societal limitations imposed upon them. Encouraging students to view themselves through a cultural lens allows them to make sense of their lives, not only as isolated individuals, but also in a social context.

Many of the women essayists maintain that they now understand how their own educational histories have been marked by their gender. Whether they were unable to speak up in class, had set limited educational goals for themselves, or doubted their abilities, they conclude that their femaleness has been the key determinant in their educational choices and experiences. Several female students relate how they trivialized their desire for an education, believing that their primary functions in life were those of wives and mothers. The title of one of the essays, "Something to Fall Back On," embodies the common rationale of higher education for women: to provide them with means of earning a living should something happen to their marriage or to their husband. Despite disappointment that their educational progress was delayed, some women essayists find that fulfilling conventional roles has strengthened them as students. One woman, for instance, concludes that her experience as a mother enabled her to learn both with her intuition and her reasoning skills.

Marginalizing aspects of a student's cultural identity may give rise to feelings of isolation that hinder academic success. The student essayists who are able to contextualize those aspects of their identity often seem to flourish academically. A white, working-class male student who habitually questions authority writes in his essay that because of his social class he had "always perceived the world with a sense of otherness, of not belonging to or being part of the status quo." Feeling excluded and doing poorly academically, he left college during his second year. When he returned several years later, he had embraced class analysis and feminism in an effort to understand his own experience; he had become an intellectual. A lesbian woman speaks of having a similar feeling of isolation that she feels impeded her studies while a young, chemical engineering student. Her fear of being open about her sexual orientation created barriers between herself and other students and faculty. Later, when she had become comfortable with her sexuality, she was able to reconnect with her peers and instructors and to learn more effectively. She also decided to change her major to economics, a field where she could "make a difference" with those social issues that had become so important to her.

Crossing cultural boundaries provokes some students to rethink their educational goals. A language barrier prompted a Japanese student to study business instead of social science as business courses involved less stringent writing requirements. Furthermore, having been exposed to different cultural and educational values than those in her native country, where "the concept of the individual is secondary to society," she has begun to focus on herself in an attempt to understand her life.

Two essays in this chapter illustrate how the juxtaposition of differing cultural perceptions and opinions in classroom discussions can enable students to change their minds and to learn from one another. An African-American male student relates how he struggled with racial issues in a graduate criminological theory course, asking himself whether in class discussions he should "avoid race altogether—just sort of discard that part of me as one would check his coat at the door of a restaurant and pick it up again upon leaving." This essay throws into high relief the absence of race as a dominant factor for interpreting one's own educational experience in many of the other essays in this chapter; it illustrates how race as a category for analysis is perceived differently by people of color as opposed to whites. The African-American students in this collection indicate that viewing themselves through the lens of race is part and parcel of who they have always been, not a newly acquired perspective. The same African-American graduate student also describes how he envied his white classmates' ability to "go about their daily lives and not be bothered so much with the issue of race." A white female student, who was initially very resistant to the issues of race and gender as discussed in a criminology class, recounts in her essay the process of "painful discoveries and personal growth" she experienced, in part, as a result of the exchange of ideas and insights in classroom debate. In her probing scrutiny, she truly illustrates the process of making sense of life through education.

The essays in this chapter enable us to understand more clearly how aspects of cultural diversity may serve as catalysts that help students redefine their identities, make sense of their life experiences in the light of a larger social context, and re-evaluate and revise their educational and career goals in more personally fulfilling directions.

≥∙

Why Should I Avoid Race Altogether?

Class had already begun as I peeked my head in the door to inquire if I was in the right place. The small group simultaneously cast their intrigued eyes upon me as I awaited a nod of confirmation. Gender-wise, it was an almost perfectly balanced group. My presence would even the score.

What was immediately evident to us all as I peered at them, and they peered back, was that I would be the only African American in the lot. Fortunately for me, however, having earned my undergraduate degree at Cornell University, I'd grown accustomed to being the sole student of color in a room full of Caucasians. This would only be another such encounter.

"Welcome to the class!" kindly asserted a white woman whose beaming smile instantly melted any tension in the air, real or imagined. "I'm Mona Danner, pull up a chair and join us!"

There was something noticeably genuine about the professor's greeting. Suddenly, I felt as if I truly belonged in her graduate criminological theory course, and that I would be free to express my unique perspective on the subject of crime and—where appropriate—race. It wasn't long after settling into the class that I would put those trusting feelings to the test.

As the discussion grew increasingly compelling, I at first hesitated to share my thoughts. For, despite the warm reception extended to me by the professor, I nonetheless sensed a certain apprehension on the part of my white classmates, who by the time I joined the class seemed to have already formed a level of comfort and cohesion. As the "new kid on the block," I very much wanted to fit in, to be liked by my peers. The only question was: At what price?

Do I ignore the fact that, as a black male, I can't help but approach the subject of criminal theory with a bit of caution and distrust? In efforts to blend in with the group, do I avoid race altogether—just sort of discard that part of me as one would check his coat at the door of a restaurant and pick it up again upon leaving?

Equally distressing was the question of balance. How much is too much sharing? Certainly it serves no one's interest to have the class agenda consumed with debates on matters of race. On the other hand, how much should I allow to go unchallenged?

"To thine own self be true" is the adage that I strive to live by. It applies both inside and outside the classroom. In accordance, I found playing the role of "model minority" unacceptable. A disruptive force I didn't care to be, but to sit idly by whilst misconceptions ran rampant was not something I was willing to do. Indeed, it was not something I could do.

Central to the success or failure of any college course is the leadership of the "head of the class"—the professor. Considering the composition of the class in question—an outspoken African-American male, an all-white peer group whose ultra-conservative political leanings were obvious to all, and a devout feminist instructor who made no apologies for her beliefs—sparks are sure to fly from time to time. As surely they did. But the most talented of educators can maintain order in what might easily, for someone less able, become chaos. We were fortunate to have such an educator.

I recall a particularly contentious exchange one evening that brought to bear all of the professor's qualities of leadership. I might add that the discussion in question sufficiently challenged my own self-restraint. Given the suggestion made by one of my wonderfully loyal Republican classmates, restraint, coupled with the wise but steady hand of a great professor, was precisely what I most needed.

On the table was a proposal to outlaw or otherwise prohibit poor people from giving birth or raising a family. The rationale, offered rather matter-of-factly, was that poverty breeds crime. Hence, if we forbid indigent people from having and raising children, then we in theory take a significant "bite out of crime," to borrow the metaphor. As perhaps the person in the class with the most intimate experience with poverty, I felt obliged to respond.

Having grown up in a single-female-headed household of five children and raised on welfare, my colleague's assertion that poverty breeds crime was a personal affront to me. Naturally, then, I confronted her on a personal level. For, had her policy been in effect prior to my conception, I would not have been around today to object to such draconianism.

I thus looked her directly in the eyes and asked if she had the moral authority to tell me I didn't deserve to be born. "Why take things so personally?!" She fired back. "You're one of the *good ones*! You're the *exception* to the rule! If the rest of *them* were like you, then we wouldn't have this problem as a society."

How rich I would be indeed if I had a dollar for every time a white person thought they were flattering me when in fact the opposite was true: You're one of the "good ones," the "exception to the rule," not like the "rest of them." To complicate matters, any effort to explain that I don't feel particularly honored by such characterization is often met with considerable friction: "Why can't *you people* simply accept a compliment without reading into it?" is the most likely retort.

As I look back in reflection on that semester at ODU, I'm reminded of the range of emotions I experienced on a weekly basis. There were times when I found the frustration of trying to enlighten otherwise very intelligent people unbearable. There were, as well, moments when I became angry just over the fact that I had to bear the burden of bringing sight to the socially blind. "Leave race out of it," my classmates would admonish me. "Race has nothing to do with anything we're discussing. This is a class about criminal theory."

So many times I struggled with an unanticipated envy. I envied the fact that my white colleagues could go about their daily lives and not be bothered so much with the issue of race. I envied the fact that they could view law enforcement in the community as a friendly presence. And yes, I envied the convenience with which they could approach a class in criminological theory, giving no care at all to racial implications—at least until I joined the class.

Though tempted many times to throw my hands in the air and simply walk away from the course, I was fortunately able to go the distance. In part, I credit my own resilience (or what some would label stubbornness) for hanging in there. I also felt deep inside that my being in the class served a purpose that far outweighed my personal discomfort. Who knows, I may have positively influenced a future policymaker or, at the very least, caused a voter to have more sensitivity to the issues of crime, poverty, and race.

My own toughness aside, I know the real sustaining force that kept me afloat was the well-deserved faith I had in our teacher. For, in the end, it was her calm presence that quieted the storms of ideological discord. It was her ability to balance compassion with assertiveness, to tolerate civil disagreement as opposed to mandating conformity, and then to employ her own vast knowledge and insight when a teaching opportunity arose which ultimately caused us all to say we benefited from the experience. What separates a mediocre teacher, in my mind, from a truly great one, is her or his ability to inspire thought and thoughtfulness in students. But be warned, one shouldn't expect to come across a great educator everyday. When you do meet one, however, it'll be an experience you'll remember for a lifetime. I was one of the lucky ones.

—Shenandoah Titus

The Words Stayed with Me

I am a twenty-seven-year-old white female working on an M.A. in public administration with a concentration in criminal justice. I was born and raised in a small village in upstate New York. Waterloo, best known as the birthplace of Memorial Day, has a population of just over four thousand. When I graduated from high school, there was one black family in Waterloo. I'm told it hasn't changed very much. Due to my parochial upbringing, I was generally unaware and unconcerned with the issues of race and gender prior to my graduate studies. I did not believe they were issues that affected my everyday life, if in fact they affected *my* life at all. My perceptions changed dramatically when I started my course work in criminal justice.

Just over a year ago, I began one of four criminal justice classes. This class was different than any I had taken before. Many previously taboo topics of conversation were now open to discussion. The issues of race and gender, along with others, were open in a way which I was not accustomed to, nor comfortable with. My upbringing and life experiences to that point had led me to believe and say that I had never been discriminated against or treated any differently because I was a woman. I also believed that race was not a major issue in everyday life, although I couldn't deny that there were some clear cases of discrimination in this country.

Before I started my first criminal justice course, I was comfortable in my classes. I participated freely and enjoyed the educational challenges each course had to offer. This class was different. An African-American male in my class spoke candidly about his race, his life experiences as a black man, and how race has numerous direct and indirect effects on all of our lives. I was uncomfortable with the things I heard, resistant to the ideas presented to me, and in denial of how race was involved in my life. Why were we frequently talking about race and gender? This was 1994, not 1964! I didn't think that either racism or sexism was representative of life today and was resentful that I was being subjected to what I considered to be useless garbage. I was as uncomfortable talking about what it was like to be white as I was listening to what it was like to be black. I, a woman, believed that the claim of gender discrimination was an excuse used by women who simply were not strong enough to succeed on their own. After all, we are all just people competing on an equal level who succeed or fail based on our own merits. I disliked much of that class. I disliked some of the students, especially the irritating black man who found a way to relate race and/or gender to almost everything. I disliked the unsettling feeling in my stomach that never went away. I later discovered that feeling was the realization that life as I knew it, comfortable and fair, blissful due to ignorance, would never be the same again.

Despite my tenacious resistance, the words from my fellow students (one in particular) stayed with me long after I left that classroom. The thoughts and feelings that were so foreign to me followed me home, to work, into my relationships, and my life as a whole. My comfortable life was suddenly troubling as I viewed it through different eyes. I began to see overt and then subtle examples of discrimination based on race and gender as it affected others. I saw how employees in the criminal justice system treated black citizens differently than whites and how this differential treatment significantly affected their lives. I was also able to recognize that women employees in the office were treated differently than men, often less respectfully and professionally.

I then began to see how *I* was treated differently as a woman, and then as a white person. Male employees, particularly those who were older than I, were less responsive to me as a supervisor than to my male counterpart, even though I was more experienced and respected in my position. I received preferential treatment over minorities in stores and restaurants, something I had never noticed before.

The most difficult part of this enlightening experience was recognizing and admitting how *I* treated people differently. I discriminated against people who were black. I am an avid runner and I enjoy running the same course in my neighborhood several times a week. I have run that course and seen many of the same people for the past two years. One day I realized that I spoke to strangers who were white with a wave, smile, or simple "Hi," but I did not speak to those who were black. I was able to recognize and admit many subtle and not so subtle ways that I discriminated against people just because of their race, more specifically, the color of their skin.

Ironically, a year after that class, after a year of painful discoveries and personal growth, I took my final criminal justice class. Again the issues of race and gender were discussed openly in the class. I was much less resistant and even supportive of these now familiar ideas. Near the end of the class, a fellow student asked a question I had heard before—Is it necessary to talk about race and gender so much? I immediately responded that it was absolutely necessary. Race and gender cannot be separated from who we are any more than we can change the fact that they affect our lives every day, including our thoughts, feelings, and actions. I am just now understanding that race and gender are important precisely because we live in a racist and sexist society; only by recognizing and confronting this can we make progress in the journey to a truly free and liberating society.

—Marie L. VanNostrand

The Education of a Southern Lady

I am a female WASP. I have always been defined by my environment and, until recently, have accepted that definition. My background is rich with southern culture and easy affluence. Because of my class, race, and gender, it has always seemed easy to do what was expected of me; I have expected it of myself. I have always gone to private schools, and I graduated from an all-girls Episcopalian boarding school. I have never had to search for myself because my class has very specific values and behaviors. If I ever faltered, I need look no further than my peers and their mothers to get back on track.

All of my teachers in high school were women from like backgrounds. Because of this unchallenging atmosphere, I have never questioned my presence within the institution of education. A southern lady's education, however, places great emphasis on etiquette and deportment in order that she may be prepared for her role in society as a wife and mother. "Hard" science and math courses were few in number because they seemed an unnecessary encumbrance for the female mind. Since high school, I have often felt that I have betrayed my class. Most of my peers went to college, found a man with the right credentials, and have gone about the business of leading their lives as their mothers did before them.

I chose a college in North Carolina where, again, everyone was the same. Having a strong family legacy at this school, I felt obliged to maintain the status quo and found that I could not. The largely Baptist, male faculty patronized me and suggested courses to me as though I were merely biding my time on the way to a "Mrs." degree. Within this country club atmosphere, I felt abrasive and unacceptable. Surrounded by so much privilege and so many niceties, there seemed to be no reason for my resentment toward the administration, the faculty, and even my classmates. My male peers were taken no more seriously; they were being trained to replicate the hegemony and questioning, critical attitudes were discouraged. After all, what more did we need to know than the fact that we were being groomed to fill our parents' shoes? Having always been told that I "belonged," I decided to try another school not so steeped in southern tradition.

I moved home and began attending Old Dominion University where I was immediately lost in the crowd and left to my own devices. My presence in any class with any teacher has been readily accepted. I have pursued a liberal arts education, probably as a byproduct of my background, and have been pleased to find that the great diversity in the student body provides for a diversity in perspectives.

Because my values and behaviors have a foundation in the elitist establishment, I have never questioned my right to do and say as I pleased in any company. I hope that this is not an ingrained sense of superiority, but rather one of established acceptance. I come to you directly from the world of the capitalist patriarchy, and my difficulties with the educational process spring not from marginalization but rather from fighting my position within the hegemony.

—Sue Ellen

My Vigour for Equality

I am from England, and I am spending one semester at Old Dominion University. I have two sisters, one older, one younger; we were brought up by our mother, who was on welfare. Most people would identify me as working class. Until I was ten years old we had no television, but spent most of our evenings listening to radio plays, sometimes telling stories, and occasionally reading; unfortunately, none of us could read too well so some of the stories became distorted in the telling. My mother loved books, particularly ones about the theater; whenever possible she would take us to Liverpool to see a ballet or pantomime.

Throughout junior school (age seven to eleven) I experienced difficulties with reading and spelling. However, I had an ability for math and I always obtained the highest class marks. Before I was to start secondary school, the Labour-run county council changed the school system, which until then had been divided into grammar and secondary modern. The grammar school was for the intelligent (mostly middle-class children with parents who encouraged them academically) and the secondary modern was the school for the rest (working-class children). The local authorities replaced this system with comprehensive schools. This meant that children of all abilities and backgrounds went to the same schools. The school officials developed a system of "streaming." In most subjects, children were placed in classes that matched their abilities. I was therefore streamed into the top classes for math, music, science, and humanities, and the lower stream for English and French. Through the streaming system, I was able to associate with middle-class children.

The teachers at my school were mostly left wing. They encouraged children of all abilities to achieve. They steered us along a fast flowing river, with the waterfalls of their ideals of equality and fairness thundering loudly against the unjust world. They encouraged discussion and radical thought. As a young, working-class woman, I came to know that my only barrier to success was my own motivation.

At fourteen, I was diagnosed as dyslexic, but because it was a relatively new concept, the school had limited means to help me. They put me in the remedial class and gave me spelling tests for about a month. My self-respect refused to allow me to stay in this group that consisted totally of people needing special educational facilities in all subjects. I refused their help and from then on decided that I had to put up with my difficulties and not tell anyone or expect anything.

At the age of eighteen, I was of two minds: to go to university, or to leave school and get a job. This decision, however, was made for me. My grandparents suggested it was about time I got a job to help my mother out. My mother's contribution to the discussion was that I should not work in a factory; she was still in a state of shock that my sis had just the year before been accepted into college to study art.

I worked for fourteen years in the financial services industry and had considerable success; however, the policy of the company was to make as much money as possible at whatever cost to its employees. I decided that I needed to find a new direction, a caring way, where people came first. I knew I had to leave the industry but had no real idea of what to do next. I had always regretted not going to university, so I decided to go. I felt I needed to do it in order to prove that I could and that I was as good as those middle-class children.

My problem and humiliation with spelling stayed with me through my working career. People either became angry at my stupidity or were insensitive, jeering and scoffing at my inability. This caused fear and distress that I have taken with me into the classroom. It is my nightmare before an exam or when I hand in an assignment. Will I fail because the instructor cannot read what I have written? This fear then extends to all other aspects of school work. Will I be able to comprehend the material? Am I overextending myself? Will I fail to obtain that degree? What am I doing here?

Within the first year of my degree course in England I asked for help with my spelling. A subsequent educational report reiterated the diagnosis of dyslexia, but also indicated that I was intelligent. This had an enormous impact on my confidence. Now when I feel challenged by either the tutor or the material, I say to myself, "Just because I can't spell doesn't mean I'm stupid."

My concern with the inequalities and exploitation I experienced in the workplace led me to study sociology. In my university in England, through discussion groups and in formulating responses to current affairs, I was able to air my views (even if they were not shared). There was a considerable difference in age between the majority of my classmates and myself. Both students and instructors expected that I, as a somewhat older student, had done the assigned reading. As a result, I found that I was beginning to dominate the discussion; at this point, I tried to wait before I spoke.

In America, I find the sociology classes difficult. I am not aware of the local issues, so I can not easily contribute. The style of teaching is class discussion form rather than lecture; there is lots of homework and many small tests. All of this reminds me of when I was in comprehensive school and brings back my fears about whether I can cope.

Students here are also different in their attitudes. They are not self-conscious about their capitalist views. They don't seem to want to acknowledge the problems within their own society. They have a callous air of indifference and hold tight to the idea that if someone is poor or in need, that is their own fault. They had the same chances; after all, this is the "Land of Opportunity." This grates against my socialist soul and against my own life experiences. As a result, I will only respond in class when in a small group and only then if I feel what I say somewhere meets what they want to hear.

Since I can remember, I have had strong feminist views. Maybe this came from living in a female-headed family or watching my girlfriends have to stay in to do housework while their brothers were allowed to go out to play. Unfortunately, when I joined the work force, my feminist views were in the minority. After many years of verbal abuse on this subject, my ego became battered. I found that my "sisters in thought" had buckled under the strain, and I no longer could find the solidarity that I needed.

My minor subject in university is therefore women's studies. The courses in that field that I am taking at Old Dominion University are developed on a mature basis: no bitty bits of homework or bitty exams. It is necessary to understand course materials and contribute in class. Assignments contain lots of reading but also present an interesting challenge. The subject matter is a part of who I am, my chalice, and, I expect, why I am living. I feel I have revitalized my faith and found again my vigour for equality.

There is one course on gender and ethics that I was (and I think still am) very wary about. It contains words and concepts that I have never been exposed to before. At one point, I was ready to get on a plane and go back to England. Then I started to read more and to understand. The course deals with a "different moral path" that women take, a path that contradicts that of traditional male thought. The subject matter intrigues me. I need to know if the inflexible management techniques and callous disregard of humanity that I witnessed, and indeed enacted on behalf of my company, are now being discussed generally as ethical issues.

—G. T. L.

Me, the Student

As students, who we are and where we come from determine how we interact in, what we bring into, and what we take from the classroom. In my case, I entered university life as a traditional white and presumably heterosexual middle-class eighteen-year-old. I am now a thirty-one-year-old nontraditional, white, lesbian, middle-class student. I was a different person then, and I now bring with me a different set of values and feelings that affects my interactions in the classroom.

Much has been said in recent years about the different quality of education males and females receive in our society. Although I am sure that, in a general way, I experienced these inequities, I do not feel as though they had a significant effect on my educational opportunities or my academic achievement thus far. I never shied away from the "hard" subjects and never felt encouraged to do so. I often think this was a result of being a "tomboy" as a child. The teachers did not apply the same gender-based standards to me as they did to many of the girls, because I did not fit neatly into the gender roles they applied. Nevertheless, I am now considered to be fairly aggressive in the classroom, outspoken, and unafraid of challenging fellow students or instructors. This is somewhat unusual in female students. In my male-dominated major, economics, my presence often introduces a different perspective to classical theory and applications.

My sexual orientation and the manner in which I have dealt with it have had a profound effect on the student I have been and am today. As a young chemical engineering student at Virginia Tech, I began to struggle with my sexual orientation. I felt disconnected from the other students and faculty in a curriculum that required a high level of group research and problem solving. Being in the closet required a great deal of evasiveness in any area involving personal interaction. This evasiveness created barriers between individuals. As I disengaged, I struggled academically, just as I was doing personally. It was only later, at Old Dominion University, when I became very comfortable with my sexual orientation, that I began reconnecting with instructors and peers. This has been important in my academic progress because I consistently perform better when I make a personal connection with the people in my classes, especially with the instructor. Now, instead of hiding in the back of the class, I make a point of being recognized. I also tend to use the classroom, when appropriate, as a vehicle for exposing heterosexual students and instructors to an "out" lesbian and to some of the issues that are important to me. This sometimes results in interesting discussions and perspectives.

Growing up in a stable, middle-class family in a mostly white school district has provided me with the social skills and communication tools necessary to interact effectively in the classroom, where rules are based on white, masculine styles of interaction. I believe that if I were black at this institution, I would have a feeling similar to the disconnected one that I had when I was uncomfortable with my sexuality. Class upbringing and racial background are often evident in a person's language and speech; if those communication tools do not fit the standard, the person will suffer academically. In this country, race and class are so closely correlated that being white has distinct advantages. Being white middle class can be a limiting experience because isolation from these problems makes understanding them difficult. During my younger years in college, I definitely suffered from this, but now I have a broader view of the world that allows me to take more from what I read and am exposed to.

So, I am a person who has enjoyed privileges and suffered disadvantages, both in life and in the classroom. The field of economics appeals to me because I am able to utilize my strong analytical abilities and to focus on the social issues that have become so important to me. When I entered college in 1979, I chose a field where I could make money; now I have chosen a field where I can make a difference.

—Lisbeth A. Freeman

On Being Myself

I was born and raised in Japan, where the individual is secondary to the society. In the United States, I find that I have placed myself in a culture where the expression of "self" is often more important. As I reflect upon my existence I find myself asking, "Where do I belong?"

In my daily work with American and Japanese personnel, I find myself caught in the middle of two cultures. As a Japanese female, I have noticed that Americans have a preconceived notion that all Japanese women are subservient and conservative. But I have always thought that my decision to come to the United States took a great deal of courage and mental strength. My American co-workers' concepts of me are incorrect, and I do not like their condescension. I thought that education might contribute to changing some aspects of my situation. Therefore, I returned to college to study more about interpersonal relationships and to further my inner quest.

Being in a different culture, I find that I have grown more quiet due to the fact that I must internally translate conversation in order to comprehend it fully. This, in turn, has caused me to talk more slowly and to be more of a thinker. I attempt to be more flexible in converting myself to an American norm. That is very difficult, and I am not always understood. Americans do not understand that their normal behavior is very contrary to my native upbringing, and I am not always aware that my culturally instilled behavior can be misconstrued. But, it has come to my understanding that there are no cultural barriers between people who are predisposed to try to bridge the culture gap through communication. I have found that the keys of logical communication are clarity and accuracy.

My work environment was another factor in my decision to return to school. I realized that it was necessary to receive a degree in order to advance my career. Since I am interested in business, human behavior, and social sciences, I wanted to be as flexible as possible in selecting my course of study. Had I been a native speaker of English, I would have chosen to study social science as my major. I believe that a business management degree encompasses many of my interests and will also help enhance my career.

My self-consciousness, my cultural background, and my work environment are essential factors to my being. Throughout the years, the experience I gain from whatever challenges I undertake will take me further toward self-realization.

—S. N.

Hungry for the Challenges of the World of Ideas

I was born in Alexandria, Virginia, in 1943, a female, the older of two children in a white, southern, working-class family. Neither of my parents attended college, and my father obtained his high school diploma by attending night school as an adult. My family did not value education for itself but only as a means to an end—as a way to earn a better living. Although my mother and father have always kept up with current events through the newspaper, neither of them are enthusiastic readers. I am not sure where I got my love of books, but they were more to me than a diversion. They were a retreat, a precious, private world of my own.

I have been an enthusiastic student with a strong inner drive to excel since first grade. Although my parents were proud of my good grades, their implicit attitude was that it did not really matter whether or not I excelled in school because my role in life as a female was to marry and raise a family rather than pursue a professional or an academic career. My gender was obviously the major factor in this attitude, but I believe working-class values that placed family solidarity above individual achievement also played a part. My parents are not anti-intellectual; they simply do not relate to academic realms of thought, and I believe they feel somewhat threatened by them. The fact that I am emphasizing women's studies in my graduate work and hold strong feminist views makes it even more difficult for them to understand my enthusiasm for my courses. They seem to think I have joined the radical fringe by embracing feminism and rejecting their traditional values.

My parents had made it clear to me when I began to talk of attending college that their financial resources were limited. My younger brother, an indifferent student, received first consideration for college money. As a male, he "needed" a college education more than I did to make a good living and support a family. However, I was determined to attain a college education, so I worked, saved my money, and obtained state teachers' scholarships to attend Radford College, which was then the women's division of Virginia Polytechnic Institute (VPI). In the 1960s, public institutions of higher education in Virginia (except the College of William and Mary) were still segregated by gender. Save for nursing students, VPI and the University of Virginia were reserved for men. I never considered an out-of-state or private school because of the expense. By carrying a larger than average class load, I was able to graduate in three and a half years with a B.S. in biology with honors. Looking back at my undergraduate years, I realize that very few of my decisions were made with clear goals in mind. I chose to follow other people's ideas about what I should do or I drifted along following the crowd. I suppose I felt that my own needs and goals were not very important.

During my senior year, it seemed to me that more of my classmates were reading *Bride's Magazine* than textbooks. Like many other women in my class, I married a few months after graduation in 1966. I then taught high school biology for two years but quit when I became pregnant with the first of my two children. I accepted the dictum that "good" mothers devoted themselves exclusively to their families and did not work outside the home unless it was absolutely necessary. For the last twenty-four years, I have occupied myself with caring for my family, volunteering, and working at a few low-paying, part-time jobs. I have also suffered bouts of deep and debilitating depression. During all that time, I dreamed of returning to school and pursuing graduate studies.

My gender, my family's class values, and my own dependence and passivity combined to limit my educational and career goals and my choices of available schools. When I entered Old Dominion in the fall of 1992, I had many insecurities about my ability to succeed as a graduate student. I was not sure whether my brain still worked, but I was hungry for the challenges and stimulation of the world of ideas. I have found that my age and my present middle-class status are advantages in my university studies. Money is no longer a major problem, and maturity and experience are conducive to success in my intellectual endeavors.

One reason I had not entered graduate school previously was that I did not wish to pursue biology further and was uncertain about what I wanted to study. As an undergraduate, I had changed my major several times because I was interested in many areas of study. For this reason, I was thrilled when I discovered the interdisciplinary M.A. in humanities program at Old Dominion. I have been drawn to the emphasis in women's studies by my life experiences and interest in furthering my understanding of feminism and gender issues.

I often wonder what I might have accomplished if I had made other choices, and I mourn for those lost contributions and achievements. At the same time I am very glad to have the present opportunity to continue my education, and I intend to make the most of it.

—Kaaren Ancarrow

What Should I Know at this Point?

What should I know at this point? Why does everyone seem to have more information than I? Why can't I retain most facts? No matter how hard I try, I cannot seem to fill all of my knowledge gaps. People say I'm bright, but they know nothing about me and how much I don't know. I am a twenty-seven-year-old white female, and I have been in school for the past twenty years. Yet I feel that I am constantly trying to catch up to others and seize something I seem to have missed—something they have. Actually, in the context of my family history, it will be a significant accomplishment next year when I will be the first of six children to complete a college degree. My siblings have found considerable success without a college education, but my quest has been in the academic realm.

My family's history is inseparable from my own. My mother, from a middle-class family, was raised to be a wife and mother. Never having seriously considered college as an option, she was forced to clean houses in an attempt to make ends meet at the end of an unhappy first marriage. My father is from a second-generation German-American blue-collar family. Despite his desire for a college education, he was convinced by family members to go to vocational high school and study electronics so that he would have a reliable trade. Following three years of mandatory military service, he became a civilian and began repairing televisions.

Since my parents were never left wanting for anything essential as children, poverty did not shape their world view. In our home, there were always books, and in addition to my parents reading to us, we witnessed them taking pleasure in reading for themselves. Many of my siblings and I developed a love of books. We had the advantage of being exposed to educational television, cultural experiences, and the natural world. My mother was involved in many school activities until she began to work full time. My parents checked and helped with our homework and both enforced the rules of standard English.

Nevertheless, the financial instability that my parents experienced attempting to raise a large family did affect my academic life. I realize now that I learned as an adolescent to cope with a hostile environment by attempting to take care of everyone around me. My preoccupation with finding ways to make everyone happy often seemed far more important to me than homework and tests. This may account for a most difficult transition into junior high school. I went from being a celebrated little "scholar" who had often been chosen to lead my fellow students to becoming a smart but less exceptional individual. I was often depressed and far less confident.

In high school, perhaps as a cry for someone to take care of me for a change or as an attempt to divorce myself from the responsibility I had taken on, I developed an eating disorder. My bulimia went undetected and unnamed for years, but it consumed me at a time when I should have been considering the importance of studies to my future. In fact, my full-fledged entry into college was significantly delayed even after my illness was diagnosed as I struggled to understand and overcome my obsession. Contrary to what was going on inside of me, people saw me as someone who had everything together. They expected that I would go to college and be relatively successful. Everyone assumed it, but no one explained what kind of choices I had or showed me how to apply to colleges. Furthermore, my parents had no understanding of the availability of financial aid.

In my junior year of high school I failed geometry, which would prevent me from receiving an academic diploma if I did not make it up in summer school. I went to my counselor for advice, and she told me that I was only going to community college and for that I didn't need SAT scores. She pointed out that I could go on the California trip I had been saving for or

I could stay home and take geometry all summer. At seventeen years of age, with no clear understanding of the ramifications of such a choice, I gladly went to California.

My experiences might also be considered a result of my gender. Developing the intellectual abilities of women is not a priority in many academic settings. Is it any wonder that I fail to find a connection to the endless litany of experiences of male writers, politicians, and soldiers that might aid me in remembering them much longer than the time it takes to complete a test about them? My own experience in classes that give value to the experiences and accomplishments of women—the classes that have given me a voice and a memory—have begun to reassure me that my inability to articulate what I intuitively know, but lack enough "facts" to prove, is a result of the very absence of women's experience and knowledge in conventional classes.

Until now, I have never had much of a vision of who I might be and the kind of life I might live. This newly developing vision is the result of my own hard work to create an education that has challenged me and met my needs despite the fact that no one has ever directly affirmed or helped me to discover my personal worth and talents. Everyday I learn how to better value myself, and I feel stronger and brighter. And still, the questions come. . . How do I fill these gaps? What is my potential? What should I know at this point? How do I compare?

—Kim Bielmann

A New Member of the Feminist Community

As a white male in modern American society, I have reaped the benefits, deserved or not, of the privilege this society gives to members of my race and gender. I have not, however, had the privilege afforded by class, and much of what I have gained has been offset by my lack of status and money. Unlike most white males, I have always perceived the world with a sense of otherness, of not belonging to or being a part of the status quo, and this has profoundly affected the way I have learned about the world.

I believe that I was probably born a skeptic, impatient with any explanation of the world that did not completely account for every possible detail and exception imaginable. Even though I grew up in a traditional family environment, influenced in part by the Southern Baptist faith, my mother instilled in me an inquisitive nature, which proved to be greatly annoying and inconvenient to most of my teachers and all whom I encountered in the church. I simply refused to accept anything that was explained away as "that's the way it has always been" or worse, "that's just the way it is." I never had the patience to hear such viewpoints or the grace to acknowledge them without showing disdain. In school and in church, I was not suffered easily by adults and not accepted readily by my peers.

As strong as this independent streak was in me, however, it did not entirely shield me from the strong influences of the culture in which I grew up or from the racial and sexist biases so prevalent in the language and society of the modern South. Nevertheless, it did not take long for me to see that white skin color and male gender did not make those who possessed them essentially better than those who did not. The transformation of my worldview from somewhat racist and sexist to self-consciously tolerant and egalitarian did not happen overnight but probably was inspired by the comparative poverty in which I grew up and the circumstances in which I lived.

I was only able to attend college because of federal grants, student loans, and my father's veteran's benefits, which made my beginning years of college very difficult. I experienced a certain amount of social isolation because of the class stratification as well as profound discomfort with the noninteractive environment of most of my classes. My grades and interest in college slumped dramatically in my second year. When I was placed on academic suspension, I left with a sense of relief rather than a sense of failure. While I do regret the opportunities that I lost, I still think that it was the best thing that could have happened to me at that time. I was in an environment where it was obvious that I did not fit in, and my expectations of college as an experience where ideas and opinions flowed freely between student and professor went unfulfilled.

Like so many different clothes, I tried on many different religions, worldviews, and philosophies, seeking those ideas that seemed to fit me best. Such idea-shopping gave me a fundamental background in learning to accept and even to celebrate diversity. I am more receptive than I am judgmental about most things that I learn, sometimes to a point of neutrality which is maddening to my family and friends. However, I am quick to adopt and unfailingly support principles which I believe to be valid and/or sacred.

Feminist thought and teachings, therefore, have had a profound effect on my world view and upon the way I learn. Previously, I had heard and questioned things and sometimes accepted them. Now, I question everything and accept little. Feminism speaks primarily to women, but it also speaks to those who have suffered from oppression, to those who feel disempowered and disenfranchised, and to those who believe that a better world can exist. The analytical and critical aspects of feminist thought have spoken strongly to me, and my response is "Yes, that's exactly it." I continually subject to a methodical analysis of content and intent everything that I have assumed or believed about the world, its histories and cultures. I examine language mercilessly, usually to the great annoyance of family and friends who are questioned and corrected aloud. I analyze the power differentials in all of the relationships in which I am involved: as a spouse, a parent, a worker, a citizen, and a student.

In the academic environment, I try to be tolerant of the perspectives, opinions, and viewpoints of others, whether I agree with them or not. However, I am quick to react in a confrontational manner to any kind of prejudice that I encounter. I get a fair amount of resistance from those who are unreceptive to conclusions derived from feminist analysis. They usually decide that I am either crazy or homosexual, or both. I also sense suspicion and sometimes hostility from feminists who are skeptical about a white male who "talks the talk and walks the walk." By now, I have become pretty much immune to either reaction, although I much prefer the acceptance and tolerance I have experienced as a new member of the feminist community.

—Tom C.

Now I Try Very Hard to Talk

At first, I was very shy in class at ODU because I came from a very small school in the country where I was never encouraged to speak up. The boys in my class were very outspoken and intimidated me. I learned not to say anything so that I would not be chastised after class. In my first college classes, I often sat in the back and didn't say a word. One day, a professor asked me a question in class that I answered correctly and very thoroughly. I shocked everyone in class with my answer. Afterwards, the professor called me aside and asked me why I never spoke. From that day on, that instructor gave me positive reinforcement and encouraged me to speak up. It took a while to get used to, but now I always try to participate and to sit in the front of the class. I am still very hesitant to speak in class because I don't want to appear stupid, but now I try very hard to talk. I do have an easier time with English or art history courses because I took so many courses like this in high school.

I don't believe that there were any particular classes I was drawn to because I am female. However, I feel that there were certain classes that I was steered away from in high school. For instance, my teachers definitely discouraged me from taking any math-oriented or technical classes. When I didn't do well in algebra, I was told that it was okay since I was a woman. Instead, my counselors tended to shift me toward home economics and English classes. I found it very difficult once I was in college to complete my algebra and calculus courses. In fact, I was so weak in those subjects that I had to take several remedial courses in order to complete what was required. I believe that since I got away from that environment and because I have a very strong mind, I did what I was told I couldn't do. If I had more money and time, I would definitely take all the courses that people told me I couldn't or shouldn't take because of my gender.

I feel like I belong in the university more than I did in high school. I am more free to choose the classes and the professors I want. I also can belong to any club I want without appearing to be a women's lib activist. I feel that I have established more of my own identity at the university. Perhaps this is because the professors listen to me and actively try to help me in most situations. I have never again been subjected to the gender stereotypes that limited me in high school.

Throughout my college years, I have learned that I can do anything that I set my mind to. I feel very confident in my abilities as a woman and am prepared for the obstacles that I will face in the future. The only thing that I can never quite overcome is the fact that when I go to my home in the country, I am looked down upon because I have gotten out and because I have finally finished my education. The men in my home town have categorized me as a "women's libber" and seem to try to find ways to poke fun at my education or my new home in the city. These are the things that I no longer have to live with constantly, and I am glad.

—P. A.

Something to Fall Back On

I am a returning student of Hispanic background, who was raised to go to college for the sole purpose of having "something to fall back on—just in case." My idea of the way my life would go was something like this: I would go to college to get my degree, meet a wonderful man, fall in love, get married, be extremely happy as a wife and homemaker, have a few delightful children, and be totally fulfilled in life.

Finding the role of Navy wife and homemaker unsatisfying, I mistakenly decided I could give my life some direction and meaning by having a child. I "knew" this would truly make me happy and was strongly encouraged by my mother to start a family. It was not until I found the role of mother to be completely lacking in all the qualities I was led to believe it would possess that I finally decided to return to school, if for no other reason than just to maintain my sanity. While there, I discovered that I actually had some worth as an individual and that doing something for my own enjoyment was very fulfilling. Finally, I decided to pursue something to truly fulfill only myself. I was searching for my identity as a person in my own right, not as someone's daughter, wife, or mother.

I do not feel that any areas were closed off to me as major fields of study. On the contrary, perhaps because of what I considered to be mostly frustrating life experiences, I felt that a plethora of educational opportunities lay before me. I was drawn to the social sciences, feeling almost a responsibility to other women, especially young women, to tell them about opportunities of which I was never told.

My ethnicity, gender, and particularly my age do affect the way that I am treated by my instructors and fellow students. I find that most instructors seem to take me a little more seriously than they do some of the younger students. I believe they have learned from experience that, for the most part, returning students are mature, focused, and serious about obtaining an education.

I have become aware that Hispanic issues are very rarely dealt with in the classroom. As a matter of fact, I have become somewhat tired of hearing only about whites and African Americans as if they were the only two groups in the world. I feel that Hispanics are not reflected in what is taught in my courses. Women are reflected in my courses, but that's probably because I am a women's studies minor. This has made me more aware of issues in other classes that I never before noticed.

I feel that my cultural identities also have something to do with why I am talkative in class. I am less afraid to talk in class than when I was younger, but I still fear speaking up too spontaneously and saying something others would consider stupid or ridiculous. I almost always think about anything I say before I say it.

My biggest frustration as I approach graduation is the prospect of graduate school. It has taken me three demanding years to finish my B.S. in psychology. Based on my performance, I feel that I am well prepared to apply to any Ph.D. or Psy.D. program. I have found these years demanding because my husband is in the Navy, and I have two young children (one is six and the other is two months old). I dealt with a lot of guilt about being away from both of them, especially since my husband has been gone the better part of these last three years. Most frustrating, as I watch my peers during the application process to graduate education, is that the only option open to me, as far as Ph.D. or Psy.D. programs are concerned, is as a full-time student. There is hardly a program in the country, let alone in the eastern Virginia area, that will take a student on a part-time basis. I am geographically limited by my family responsibilities. I can't believe this is not considered discrimination. I know many returning women students who have no choice or desire but to pursue their educations on a part-time basis. It seems to me that a lot of women are prevented from pursuing their educational goals. The communities which might be served by these women miss out on the benefits of employing someone with a great deal of life experience.

As for me, I have decided to take a few years off and devote myself to spending time with my family. I will probably pursue some graduate courses in a master's program since I don't want to return to school full time right after having had my second child. As far as the doctorate, it will have to wait until my children are older or my husband gets out of the Navy.

—M. L. S.

Beyond the Fairy Tale

My gender (female), has affected the nature of my studies more than anything else. Even at a very early age I remember feeling uneasy, plagued by the notion that I was expected to do well in school—but not *too* well—lest I appear unattractive to the boys or threaten to overpower them. I was the beneficiary of an upper-middle-class upbringing and had loving, highly educated parents who encouraged me to explore the world of academia, introduced me to liberal ideas, and exposed me to many valuable cultural experiences. They could also afford to send my four sisters and me to private, liberal arts colleges, and being white, no doors were closed to us. However, beneath the surface of all of this extraordinary opportunity lay the unspoken message: "Your *real* vocation will be to support a loving husband and his children, so whatever you study is secondary." Thus I never took my future nor my ability to make my way in the world alone too seriously, and neither did my teachers nor my mother, who committed herself primarily to the nurturing of her family, as did many women of her generation.

It wasn't until I was thirty-eight (in 1982) and my youngest son was in school all day that I began to doubt that the fairy tale I'd been raised on could bring me the fulfillment that it had promised. Why *didn't* I feel content and why *weren't* the roles of wife and mother, which defined me, enough? The seeds of doubt began to grow, and, feeling the loss of any children to nurture full time, I was propelled out into the world to seek an identity beyond motherhood to define me; at thirty-eight I was beginning the process of self-discovery which I should have been engaged in two decades earlier. That year, four things happened which changed the direction of my life: I took a job at a tennis club which gave me money of my own, enrolled in a writing course, met Marilyn (a staunch feminist), and read Doris Lessing's story, "Room Nineteen." I soon read almost all of Lessing and began work on my M.A. in English; fueled by Marilyn's ideas and the works of women authors who echoed the silent yearnings within my own heart, I was inspired and strengthened to redefine myself as a woman. I admit I listened most attentively to the ideas of female teachers, began to treat other female students with greater deference, and to take myself seriously as a student for the first time. This process led me to challenge the basis of my marriage, which was more traditional than egalitarian, to confront my own personal issues in therapy and, eventually, to study for an M.S. in psychology. A year ago, when my youngest son left for college, I was once again driven by a shift in my identity as a nurturer to seek a new dimension in my life. I gravitated, once again, to the ideas and company of women studying feminist ideas, in an effort to further understand myself.

I find it ironic that it has been largely through the disillusionment of the fairy tale I was fed as a young girl that I have been driven to seek so many answers which have enriched my life as a woman. The pain of a lack of true intimacy in my marriage led me to confront both marital discontent and, eventually, to deal with my own, deeply buried issues. It was also the pain of loss as my children grew and needed me less that forced me out into the world to seek new fulfillment. In both instances, it was the unfulfilled promise of the fairy tale which led me to take the risks which eventually led to the two things

I desired most: a truly intimate, egalitarian marriage, and a sense of self totally separate from the roles of wife and mother which had always defined me.

I also find it ironic that it was the experience of becoming a mother, a part of the fairy tale I embraced, which gave me the confidence and courage to begin to take those risks which led to so many positive changes in my life. It wasn't until I became a mother that I fully understood the meaning of true intimacy. Mothering also made me feel powerful—I was in charge! It forced me to rely on my instincts for the first time, not just my thoughts. When I returned to the classroom as a graduate student, my competence as a mother gave me confidence. Thus I began to learn more creatively, as a woman, instead of trying to emulate male students as I had done before. Today, as a student I feel that I benefit from my race, class, *and* gender because I have finally learned to embrace, rather than to reject, my uniquely female power.

—Jean Caggiano

Woman, Mother, and Nurse

I am a woman, a mother, and a nurse; many believe that caring and nurturing are natural for women and mothers and that these three words are synonymous and interchangeable. However, my sex was determined at conception, whereas I did not become a mother until I was twenty-eight. Furthermore, it took me years of study and the completion of an extremely difficult course of studies, followed by a state registration examination, to earn the title of nurse. Nursing is an art which takes years of practice to perfect. Compassion may provide the motive to care for the sick, but knowledge acquired through formal education is the working power of the professional nurse. I learned the principles of nursing in the classroom, but the art was developed at the bedsides of the sick and dying. I had to hurdle many obstacles to become a nurse, and it is a wonder to me that I was able to graduate from college. My success in the classroom allowed me to develop into an independent, self-supporting woman.

I grew up in the rural South—poor, white, and female. The first school I attended was a three-room building where two female teachers taught first through fifth grades. The "Book-mobile" brought us books, and each student was allowed three books a week. Joy and anticipation are the earliest feelings I can recollect about school. Reading and books provided me with an escape from and a way to cope with life. Through books, I envisioned a different life for myself, a life of college, career, and independence. However, education was costly, and I had no financial resources. Through good grades and academic performance, I earned a full scholarship for college. Marriage, teaching, and nursing were the only career paths presented to me in high school. I became a nursing student because I did not want to be a teacher, and I certainly had no desire to marry at that time.

Philadelphia General Hospital School of Nursing (Block-ley) accepted me for the class of 1962. I grew up very fast that first year. Nursing classrooms were centers of didactic learn-ing. Professors lectured, students took notes and memorized them. The hospital wards were the laboratory of learning and practice. Student nurses spent forty hours a week on the hospi-tal units in addition to their heavy course work. This female-dominated education provided me with technical skills to nurse, administrative and leadership skills, and provisions for professional advancement.

My white skin provided me privileges that I would not recognize until much later. I grew up in the segregated South with separate schools and separate water fountains. I thought crossing the Mason-Dixon Line would eliminate discrimina-tion. I was wrong; Blockley had few black pupil nurses or graduate nurses. The city of Philadelphia prided itself on hav-ing Mercy Douglas Hospital to provide nurses' training to African Americans. I remember thinking, "This is not different from the segregated school system I left." Philadelphia Gen-eral Hospital's student body was overwhelmingly female, white, Anglo-Saxon, and Protestant. Social status or class ori-gin did not appear to affect success. The school provided room, board, uniforms, and laundry service. Everyone looked the same. Hard work, not family origin, provided school sta-tus.

Hospital-based education for nurses succeeded in produc-ing competent, skilled practitioners. There were opportunities to practice every procedure hundreds of times. The basic science courses of chemistry, biology, microbiology, anatomy, and physiology were taught well. However, this system, with all its advantages, did not tolerate creativity; I learned to stuff feelings, hide my critical thinking, and conform. I learned these lessons well, and it took me more than twenty years to unlearn them.

Nursing and caring are what I do best, but society does not value highly these abilities. I believe them to be essential for a high quality of life. My nursing education taught me how to take care of others but not of myself. In the classroom at ODU I am developing a concept of womanhood that affirms, values, and nurtures me. The graduate-level liberal arts courses in which I am enrolled have strengthened the true spirit of nursing in me and are providing me with new information, bringing to life essential parts of me that have been dormant.

Five years ago, I returned to the study of music after denying myself that pleasure for a long time. I feel that my return to the classroom for graduate work is like my return to music. The classroom has provided music and nourishment for my soul.

—Gale Garner

First-Generation American

I was born in Colorado Springs, Colorado, to parents of Latvian descent who immigrated to the United States in the late 1940s. It was not until I started school that I found out that I was different and that other children did not want to play with me because I could not speak English. This inability was an anomaly to them and devastating to me. My parents were prosperous enough to provide me with a language tutor, so that I soon became integrated into the classroom, but my sensitivity to being different from my peers haunted me in school for years afterward.

Eagerness to fit in with classmates, combined with the common female pattern of self-consciousness in the classroom, made me more social than scholarly in high school. I did what teachers told me to do just so I could go off with my friends to football games, dances, and other activities. My desire not to stand out from the crowd made me feel ambivalent toward the Japanese-American students in school who were present because a World War II detention camp had been located nearby. While I could relate to these students because of the language difficulties experienced by some of them, I could not afford to violate the prevailing high school code which looked upon them as outsiders and labeled anyone who spent time with them as deviant.

My parents made my decisions about university for me. Their ethnic background and their desire for me to improve upon their opportunities and options pushed me into a course of study about which I felt lukewarm. Those college years were very difficult for me. As a young woman without a strong sense of my own abilities, I was vulnerable to the indifference and sometimes outright discrimination toward female students that was common in college classrooms in those days. I anxiously awaited graduation because I thought that the working world would be different. How wrong I was. The discrimination and humiliation of those college years continued.

It was not until I decided to return to the world of academics at the age of forty-plus that I discovered how damaged my self-esteem really was. At first it was even difficult for me to uncover what my interests were. When I found my way into a women's studies course, I finally found topics which spoke to me and a classroom atmosphere in which I felt comfortable raising my hand and expressing an opinion.

Even this sense of fit has not assured an easy transition into academics. I had been spoon-fed knowledge by most of my undergraduate teachers. I swallowed it and then regurgitated it, not really absorbing the true meaning of what I was learning. The information which they passed on to me never stayed with me; I now have to go back and relearn it. Because I was still guided in those undergraduate years by my fear of being singled out, I rarely asked questions or volunteered information. My passivity in the classroom assured that I never acquired analytic skills. It is still very difficult for me to summarize what I read and to perceive themes and assumptions in texts.

My early schooling, combined with my first-generation

sense of not quite belonging, has left me with educational self-esteem so low that, to this day, I have a great deal of difficulty in completing assignments for fear of being criticized. This struggle will most likely stay with me for many years to come. Although I do have a voice now, I am still fearful of not being perfect.

—Brigita Silins

Regaining My Spanish Heritage

My name is James Gracia and I am a male Hispanic student at Old Dominion University. I was born in Barcelona, Spain, and my parents and family moved to the United States when I was seven years old. My first language was Spanish, and it is still the primary language we speak at home. My parents came to the United States in search of a better life for themselves and our family. I remember from a very early age my father stressing to me the importance of learning the English language and becoming familiar with American culture. His thinking was that this was essential in attaining success in the United States. Consequently, most of my school-age life was spent at boarding schools in the New England area, while my older brothers remained in Virginia working in the family business.

I remember as a young student the horror of entering school and facing a classroom with my limited command of the English language. I was usually a very able and outgoing youngster, but in the classroom, I was much too uncomfortable to even open my mouth. In fact, I had one teacher who tried to keep me back in the third grade because he thought I was stupid. The truth was I understood all the material perfectly well; I just had a hard time verbalizing it in English. If others had made me more comfortable speaking my broken English, I would have learned it more quickly. That is why I take extra care to try to befriend and to put at ease the foreign exchange students I encounter in class. I just wish others would do the same. As I was growing up, my father insisted that I go by the surname Grace instead of by my real last name, Gracia. His reasoning was that Gracia was too confusing for Americans to pronounce and spell. It was not until I entered the university that I went back to my original last name, Gracia.

Much to my father's chagrin, I have chosen Spanish and philosophy as my fields of study. It was my father's dream that I be the one to take over the family business, but that is just not going to happen. All that study and all that schooling backfired on him as my instructors and my friends encouraged me unconditionally to pursue what interested me most. Furthermore, I wish to regain some of the Spanish culture I missed out on growing up. It is my hope to major in Spanish studies and then go to Spain to live for a while. After all, I have relatives in Spain whom I have never even met.

At the university level, I have experienced, for the most part, unconditional acceptance and encouragement from fellow students and professors. In fact, they are responsible for helping me to find the confidence to pursue my goals. However, I do have some friends within the university who affectionately refer to me as "wetback" or "chinchilla breath." I realize that it's all in good fun, but it's still disconcerting at times. For the most part, I let these statements roll off my back like the waters of the Rio Grande.

—James Gracia

4

In Search of an Education

ॐ

Introduction

What does it mean for a student to envision an education? Are the educations students seek purely the result of individual inclinations and abilities? Or do their cultural backgrounds, as interpreted by the students themselves, influence their visions of an ideal education as opposed to the "realistic" aspirations urged upon them by others? Do students utilize their experiences as members of these diverse groups in making academic decisions? The student essays we have collected in this final chapter of *Ourselves as Students* provide us with some intriguing and enlightening answers to these questions. In this chapter, all sixteen student essayists interpret their educational experiences through the lens of their particular cultural identities and life experiences. This provides us with an unusual look at a virtually hidden—and we believe until now unidentified—process of integration by which students arrive at their academic planning and decision making.

More than half the essays in this chapter are written by nontraditional students who have attended at least one other college or university before coming to Old Dominion. These students appear to increase their knowledge about their intertwined social and educational identities by comparing classroom experiences between institutions. In turn, they use this information to enlarge their view of suitable educational approaches and choices. Traditional students, on the other hand, seem to compare college to high school in an attempt to gain a similar vantage point. In either case, the students writing here look closely at how particular courses and disciplines, certain professors and teachers, and university and school communities as a whole pay attention to their diverse needs.

How, then, do students come to understand their socially constructed identity as an integral part of their educational identity, and how do they manage to devise academic strategies and methods based on this knowledge? The essay "Keeping My Focus," written by a mature undergraduate, provides one example of how a student engages in this decision-making process. A mixture of gender, ethnic, and class factors served to discourage her from considering a college education or from even thinking herself intelligent. Choosing the military as an alternative, she did not revise her conception of herself or her aspirations until a tentative try at a college psychology course taught her that she was far from dumb. This new information pushed her to reevaluate herself and her previous educational experiences and resulted in her attending school full time. She reveals a personal transformation as she describes her determination to teach children, for childhood "is an important time in the development of their confidence," and she hopes "to prevent someone else from delaying or abandoning their dreams." Another student, once driven out of college on gender grounds by a belittling professor, has enrolled in a graduate program at ODU to prepare herself for work about which she truly cares. More confident now, and more astute about the obstacles facing women, she is still shaken by the vaguely harassing remarks and actions made by one of her professors. This time, however, she refuses to drop out of school because her educational goals are firmly fixed to life work in which she believes.

Students like these often must make difficult educational choices because of their life circumstances. The individual and personal realities of students' lives provide much of the backdrop for this chapter as they do for most of this book. In this chapter, however, we can see how students develop an oppositional educational strategy in response to many different forms of adversity. This approach seems to arise when students, like the two mentioned above, are able to reaffirm their abilities and self-worth in the face of the negative consequences of certain educational encounters and cultural expectations. These consequences, which include deferred dreams, lost opportunities and diminished accomplishments, provide students with strong resolution and the basis for a retaliatory strategy that allow them to reengage the educational process in a new and dramatic fashion.

There are also more traditional students who are in search of an education, or perhaps it is more accurate to say there are students who are in search of a more traditional education. The attempts to accommodate the viewpoints and needs of a greater array of students than ever before and the tendency in some courses to put the emphasis on questioning received wisdom rather than on imparting established truths make some students uncomfortable and irate. This is not what they had envisaged when they planned for a university education. Such a reaction is exemplified by the essay written by a young white man who describes himself as both a mechanical engineering major at ODU and a part-time student "attending the Limbaugh Institute for Advanced Conservative Studies." This undergraduate student laments his treatment in classes where, he says, he must resist "*creative revision of accepted principles.*" Although this student's essay has a facetious tone, he nonetheless makes the point clearly: he resents the attention given to diversity at the university, because in his view it has replaced an emphasis on "accepted principles." To rectify what he sees as an unbalanced curriculum and flawed education, he argues for a "department of conservative studies."

Two other essays that incorporate some of these same themes offer us diametrically opposed views of what goes on in the classroom. They raise the question of how students interpret and respond to what they hear in class and, hence, what they derive from their educational experiences. The white author of "On Guard Before I Speak," bemoans the constraints on classroom speech imposed by the fear of offending someone in courses that deal with gender or race. Where he worries that this fear keeps the truth from surfacing, a black female student in another essay describes her concern that the knowledge and expertise of black professors are discounted by many students. While he describes a fear of being silenced, she reports that she has observed disruptive and disrespectful behavior on the part of white males in their efforts to silence a black female instructor who tries to correct common misconceptions about race voiced by students in her class.

The complex constellation of social variables that each student brings to the classroom intersects with the educational curriculum and practice that they find in place, thereby determining a student's educational ideology. An array of educational visions can arise in response to these ideological strategies. There are several essays in this chapter that share the common boundary of such strategies, but seem to give rise to divergent ideological visions.

An older, white engineering student asserts in his essay that "the university is a tool that one uses to further their career." We learn the degree to which he has defined his educational needs as he goes on to say that he "dislikes the university imposing certain requirements in order to make me a better person." In another essay, a black woman activist and graduate student gives a sense of a different educational ideology, which she describes in these terms: "I learned that a college degree cannot shelter you from the storm. It never has and it never will. Racism will not let me forget who I am." Later in her essay we catch a glimpse of her educational vision: "My people taught me the essence of perseverance, strength, and accomplishment; and I will never forget why I am here." It appears that the educational visions of these two students are as varied as the unique social and educational identities from which they arise.

As we read about the highly individual and diverse educational needs of the students writing in this chapter, we cannot help but become acutely aware of the immense challenges that the university will face as it attempts to re-vision its own purpose in the face of the changing visions of its students.

Fearing Our Own Voices

"Why was Jan apologizing to me for speaking up in class? Why was Kenny always talking when it was obvious that he hadn't read the week's assignment? I see everyone waiting patiently for Kenny to stop talking . . . then they sigh, lean on the table, look around, then turn to me to stop his madness. Yet when I do intervene and tell him it is time to hear from someone else, the women step cautiously out of their silence, darting glances toward Cal and Tom to make sure that they don't have something to say first. I take the opportunity to say a name—Maggie, what did you think about this—and Jan speaks up, apologizing to the class that she feels as if she's always talking."

That paragraph comes from a journal that I am keeping this semester while I am serving as a graduate teaching assistant, facilitating a discussion group. It is strange to be dealing with issues of silence among undergraduate women while I still remember so vividly my own struggles to break through the barrier of silence that paralyzed me in the classroom for so many years.

My journal entry goes on to describe a discussion some of the women students and I had after class that day. "After class, I talked about issues surrounding silence with Pam and learned that she has a fear of sounding stupid, of not connecting her thoughts to her words, of not making sense and of dominating the class. Maggie, joining our conversation, expressed the same fear of not making sense. Why do so many women fear this? Is it because the language used within the walls of higher education intimidates and excludes women? Is it because they are so used to not being heard at all in other classrooms that the thought of frequently joining discussions in this class completely overwhelms them? One thing is clear, not one of us has escaped socialization as females in the classroom and we are all having to fight vigorously to overcome it."

I remember well the day that I myself turned from looking

out the window to look at my instructor and actually understood and identified with the world she was introducing to us. It was on that day that I discovered the importance of not just belonging to an academic setting, but contributing to it. The instructor did not lecture endlessly at us; she spoke to us. She did not want us to take extensive notes so that we could memorize and regurgitate information. She asked us to do what every other one of my instructors had failed to do in the past: she asked us to think and share our opinions. That is why, for the first time, what was happening in the classroom became more interesting to me than what was happening outside.

I did not really start my education at the university until that day. Most of my experiences in the classroom contributed to my insecurities about education. I had begun to convince myself that I did not belong in an institution of higher learning. The fact that I am white certainly gave me the advantage of blending in with the other students, but being female and from a lower-income family prevented me from feeling as though I were a part of academia. Being female alone would not necessarily perpetuate this anxiety, but coming from a lower class as well certainly influenced the way others perceived me and how I had learned to see myself. My family consists of incredible people, but they have only known hard work and survival. They were not able to prepare me for the language used in the classroom. Consequently, I avoided participating in class for fear of pronouncing names or words wrong or having the professor ask me a question using words I did not know. It seemed as though everyone else had been exposed to twice the vocabulary I had been. I was too ashamed to admit that I didn't understand many of the words I heard around me. After all, wouldn't they think I was stupid? It was this same fear that prevented me from talking to my professors after class or during their office hours.

It has been a few years since that day I turned from the window and began the struggle to overcome my fear of contributing to class discussions and although I am not completely outspoken, I have managed to break through that paralyzing barrier of silence. Now, however, I see it carried on in those younger than I who are my students. As a female student, I keep in mind the need to overcome the fear of my own voice, and as an apprentice teacher, I remind myself never to forget that I was once one of those intimidated, frightened, and silent persons in the classroom.

—C. Blue

I Move Through Text with the Flexibility of Ribbon

I am twenty-three, white, and female. I grew up poor, raised by a divorced mother, and surrounded by people who were high-school educated at best. My mother never asked if our homework was done, but she was adamant that our chores be completed. I was influenced in childhood by people who worked the land or did other forms of manual labor. For these people, higher education appeared impractical and an escape for those who could not handle real work. That was fine with me, because thinking is hard. I did my school assignments haphazardly and put forth very little effort. The practical learning that I saw all around me—operating a tiller, assembling an engine, baking perfect desserts, training horses—was invalidated by the educational system.

At the age of sixteen, I was transported to a world where higher education meant survival. I moved in with my father (who belonged to a different social class), and I began attending a very competitive high school. I, however, was in no position to compete; I had no study skills and no background in many courses. In this situation, I drifted toward English as a subject. I did not need the kind of base for English that would have been required for science or math where one class was needed to learn another. In English, I did not seem to need basic knowledge, other than the ability to read. There was also less need for competition in these courses and more room for subjectivity and a multitude of viewpoints.

Eventually, I learned study skills, and in my new world, it was expected that I would go on to college. The culture of which I was now a part sent signals to me that if I got an education, I would have a place to use it. I was given a sense of belonging in other ways as well. Not only were all my teachers white like I was, but I developed a learning style of bonding with the material that I read. Because I was often reflected in what I read, I felt a closeness to it and had an emotional stake in it. This pushed me to work harder.

In high school, there were other ways, having to do with gender, in which English seemed more and more to be a suitable subject for me. For one thing, the boys and girls in heterosexual couples did not compete with one another, and math and science belonged to the boys. For another, since gaining male approval was so important to me and to many of my female friends, I had fantasies of a male teacher showing me special attention. The male teachers in English always seemed more romantic than those in other subjects. The search for male approval in high school held more importance for the females I knew than choosing a subject that might make a profitable and interesting career.

When I got to the university, I began to realize that while I may be reflected as a white person in what I read, I often am not reflected as a female or at least as women with whom I feel kinship. Lady Macbeth or the women of *The Great Gatsby* were not easy for me to identify with. I did not really see myself as consumed with greed or frivolity. I treated these female characters as lessons as to what I should not be. I found it necessary to go one extra step to translate the text in search of a way to identify with it, much like one does with a parable. This skill has proved enormously useful in my literature track at the university. I can move through text with the flexibility of ribbon. If I can translate a male perspective to fit my own, I can translate cultural differences, time settings, age, political agendas, and more. The layers are endless.

Whatever the reason, it has appeared to my professors that I have a talent in literature, so I have been encouraged to study it. My true attachment to literature did not come, as far as I am concerned, until I involved myself in women's studies, which interested me because of my gender. In women's studies, I developed the skills to take translations and dismantle them further. I discovered infinite maps within texts, and rather than searching solely for my own identification, I learned to look for other hidden roads, subverted voices. I feel community and relationships in texts. I combine these skills with what I have come to believe, based on my childhood in a rural, working-class community, that no form of knowledge is invalid. I trust what I see, what I learn, even if it is not traditionally accepted knowledge.

—Michelle Angus

I Resist C.R.A.P.

The topic of bias based on gender, race, creed, or sexual orientation is currently of great interest in the university community. As a student at Old Dominion University, I feel as though I am treated fairly in most respects. I am an Irish-American male, eighteen years old. I am middle-class and come from a quiet suburban background. I was educated in public schools from kindergarten through twelfth grade.

I am a mechanical engineering major. That choice had nothing to do with gender, race, or class. It was due instead to economic factors. The world, becoming increasingly technological, will need many engineers and many computer scientists in the future. Like any good American, I hold my personal finances in high regard. For this reason, flipping burgers full-time, nursing, and teaching are out. So is social work. After all, we have the national health care plan to take care of illegal aliens, Rodney King, our children, and our wallets.

Some people feel that certain occupations are closed to them because of their ethnic heritage. I feel their pain. As an Irishman, I find that such occupations as dockwork and bricklaying are closed off to me, but then again, they do not offer sufficient compensation to satisfy my donut cravings.

The question has been raised: Do you feel that you are reflected in the classes taught [at this university]? The simple answer is no. That is why I also attend the Limbaugh Institute for Advanced Conservative Studies part-time. At the Limbaugh Institute, my political tendency towards common sense and morality is much more in evidence. At ODU, a good academic environment prevails in the classroom if not in the dorms, and after all, classes are about learning material, are they not? As a student, my ethnic, religious, and social background are of little relevance to most teachers outside the English department.

In English class, I am somewhat resistant to listening to the rantings of various leftists whose work is included in my textbook. This is due in part to race; being white, it is somewhat depressing to be reminded of my tremendous racial guilt, which if allowed to build up, can lead to uncontrollable fits of kowtowing to liberals wherever they can be found. I prefer to avoid this condition when possible, since it can lead to sudden and unexplained changes of traditions and lifestyle. My resistance to *c*reative *r*evision of *a*ccepted *p*rinciples (c.r.a.p.) is also traceable to my political orientation.

I have said that I feel I am treated fairly in most respects. There is one area in which I have been a victim of harassment in the past, however. It has to do with . . . my orientation. Yes, it happens. This situation is only beginning to come out of the closet, and I'm proud to be part of bringing it out. Every day, conservatives on college campuses across the USA are politically harassed—subjected to remarks from professors and other students that are demeaning to their political orientation. I believe that this is wrong. In America, we do not discriminate on the basis of race, sex, creed, or lifestyle. We should not be discriminated against because of our political orientation either. Our administration has not done anything that I am aware of to address this egregious situation.

This is the area where I feel that my rights are trampled on a daily basis. Conservatives, like everyone else, deserve a learning environment that is free from images and speech which demean and insult us. It is very difficult, for example, for a conservative to maintain his/her self-esteem in the face of reading biased textbooks such as mine, which includes only one conservative essay among over eighty liberal works. This trend extends to class participation, where conservatives are infrequently asked to answer questions or join in class discussions. Even ODU's mascot, Big Blue, is a liberal symbol. As a lion, Big Blue represents Africa, where lions are found, and thus Afrocentrism. Big Blue, then, is a symbol of oppression to largely European-descended conservatives, who must silently endure the cheering crowds of liberal students led by our mascot. Conservatives are assaulted in the halls every day by posters proclaiming liberal causes, while our own activities and causes are subject to review in case of insensitivity.

I feel that it is time for an end to this slavery. There should be a department of conservative studies. The honor council should look into incidents of political harassment. Don't believe it happens? You've probably harassed someone today already. All liberals are potential harassers. Just wait until you are nominated for the Supreme Court.

—S. M. M.

The Many Faces of Me

Paula Giddings, a black historian, asked herself the question, "When and where do I enter?" in her journey towards self-realization as a black woman. I, too, have asked that question of myself. Who am I? I am a woman who has found herself to be a traditionalist, pessimist, misogynist, and all of the other ist(s) that have kept me from my own personal liberation. Yet, through the diverse experiences of my life, I have evolved into a feminist, realist, social activist, and an optimist. I love what I have become, though I am constantly evolving. My childhood and my college experiences definitely have had a profound effect on my life.

I am the product of a working-class family where it was always implied that education was the key to liberation, but no one ever really told me that it would take more than just a piece of paper with two letters on it. As a child, I always felt that my parents, in their struggle for survival, attempted to shield me from the harsh realities of racism and classism without realizing how damaging their actions were.

It was very difficult for my parents to discuss the obstacles they hurdled as black people living in a white-dominated world. My parents felt that education would protect me from the injustices they faced. Somehow, I would jump right into another economic class and would be able to "get a good paying job" and to close my eyes or, should I say, "my front door" to racism and classism. However, that was not the case.

Painfully, I learned that a college degree cannot shelter you from the storm. It never has, and it never will. Racism will not allow me to forget who I am. What I really needed from my parents was the truth—the truth about their struggles—what it was like to protest for what you believe in, how injustices not only have to be publicly protested but changed. Their stories would have been my shield.

My primary and secondary schooling never dealt with the issues of race and class. Everything I read was from a white perspective. The history taught to me did not embellish contributions made by blacks or other persons of color. For this reason, I read voraciously about black history as a child and throughout my schooling attempted to identify with my culture.

Equally disturbing were my family's values. My father was very traditional in his thinking. A woman's place was in the home, performing domestic duties. Although my mother worked, she echoed his beliefs by her actions. She cleaned, cooked, and ironed, without much support from him. My sisters and I were also expected to share in the domestic responsibilities. I was always uncomfortable with the fact that my father felt that his position as the "head of the household" exempted him from joining us in the cleaning and the ironing. In my opinion, men and women are supposed to equally participate in household chores.

In my house, it wasn't the question of what you would be doing after high school, but what college you would be attending. My sisters and I all knew that since our parents never finished college, we would have to fulfill their dreams. I chose Howard University because I wanted to have what some have called the "black experience"—to be in an environment that fostered black achievement and cultural awareness, which was very key in defining who I was and aspired to be.

At Howard, the classroom was not only a laboratory for the creation and exchange of ideas, but a place to raise and question issues relating to race, class, and history. My mind was constantly challenged at every turn. No longer did I accept what was forced upon me by my family and school system. However, there were several things which disappointed me during my matriculation at Howard. All over the campus there were attitudes of elitism, sexism, and racism. If you had money, clothes, or were the "right" shade, you were revered. No one really wanted to talk about it, but I did.

Moreover, I was shocked by the lack of discussion surrounding the black woman's experience throughout history. Black men were always the victors, the activists, the central figures of change. So, I began to research about my sisters—what they did and who they were. They were more than just mothers—breadwinners, activists, freedom fighters, and much more—and I began to embrace a new consciousness as a black woman.

Much has happened since my graduation from Howard. There have been jobs, people, lovers, friends, politics, movements, and many experiences which have shaped my life. Each situation brings a new piece to the puzzle, and I am grateful because I believe that women can learn from all of their experiences.

I do not feel uncomfortable as a student at ODU. Even when I am the only person of color in my classroom, it does not concern me. Blacks have always been equipped to deal with obstacles. I suppose I inherited this "gift" as a beneficiary of the civil rights movement. My people have taught me the essence of perseverance, strength, and accomplishment, and I will never forget why I am here. Ultimately, I have made the decision in my life to explore and to refine my understanding of that which I feel to be oppressive as I continue on my journey to become physically, spiritually, and mentally whole.

—Ezell L. Battle

As a Black Woman

I was born in Queens, New York, nineteen years ago. My mother was still in college, and my dad was in the Air Force. I am the younger of two children, and my brother, who is three years older, was born in England. After my parents' divorce, my mother, brother, and I moved to Freeport, Long Island, a suburban town. While raising two children, my mother managed to continue her education, and she now holds a Ph.D. in social work. She has placed a high value on education, and that is what brought me to Old Dominion University.

As a black woman attending a predominantly white university, I feel a certain amount of pressure from my peers, professors, and, of course, my mother, to achieve academic excellence. I have been forced to study things that will benefit me, but I also feel that I have been denied the opportunity to take courses which include the representation of blacks. I am required to take some kind of history as a general education course, and a black history course is not acceptable for fulfilling that requirement. How can Americans, both black and white, become unified if the educational system is geared toward white Americans and not Americans as a whole? It is impossible to understand the black American heritage if one is not taught about black existence from the beginning of American history.

Even though I am not part of the majority here at the university, I feel that I was well prepared for the challenges that I have faced and will continue to face. Being raised by an educated parent, in a white neighborhood, has been one of the key factors.

In the North, I had rarely been subjected to racial conflicts, and attending school in the South has been quite an experience. I have become friends with a lot of people who, having grown up in the South, have experienced many racial conflicts and dislike whites. I have also met a lot of white people who have grown up in prejudiced homes and are finding it hard to adapt to society as it exists now.

I believe that curiosity has a lot to do with how professors and peers treat black people. All my life I have been what they would call a "token nigger" because I was always one of the few blacks who were in honors classes and clubs. At Old Dominion University, white people always look to me to answer questions and respond to issues dealing with blacks. I am always asked my opinion on racial issues because I am one of the few blacks in most classes. This is very upsetting to me because my being black doesn't mean that I can relate to everything that has happened to other black people.

Therefore, I believe that improvements in regard to race,

gender and other sources of discrimination have to begin at the educational level. If educated people are still naive about race relations, how can we expect uneducated people to understand?

—Lavonne

Right Now I Am Poor

I am a twenty-five-year-old female undergraduate student. I consider myself black, although I am bi-racial (my mother is white). I come from a middle-class working background. I am the single parent of a three-year-old boy.

Right now I am poor. It is difficult to find the money to go to school. I do qualify for grants and loans, but of course loans have to be paid back. I returned to ODU two years ago after an approximate eight-year absence. Since my re-enrollment, I have tried very hard to bring my GPA up so I can compete for a scholarship. My GPA is currently a 3.5, but it still may not be high enough to earn a scholarship.

Not having money to attend school has had a big impact on my life. Everyone knows how much time, energy, and effort is put into applying for and receiving financial aid. Sometimes, I think one should qualify for three credits just for successfully dealing with financial aid. I feel the university takes advantage of students with financial needs. Last semester, I was under the impression that I would receive the remainder of my loan money before the Christmas holiday. I had planned to use my money not only for my rent and my other bills but also to buy a Christmas tree for my son and a few gifts. Even though my loaning institution sent the check to ODU on December 12, I did not get my money until February.

A friend told me that the university deposits all the loan checks and draws interest on them for at least a month. I do not know if this is true, but it is an infuriating thought. Students like me need the money they borrow for very urgent things. Yet, the school has total control of when the money is distributed. And of course, they get their money first, not to mention any interest that may result from depositing the checks. I feel this is unfair.

When I was a freshman (age sixteen), I took a history

course at ODU. The professor, who was white, tried to tell my class that slavery in America wasn't as bad as it had been made out to be. I spoke up and disagreed but few other students did, and I was just about the only black person who objected. I purposely chose to refute this professor's view in my term paper. I got a C on the paper, and I still believe it was because this particular professor was biased.

I am a very open-minded, liberal person. I feel obligated to help teach others about race relations and to dispel stereotypes and racial misconceptions when I hear them in class. I hope that someone will learn something from me and I from them, when such discussions are held in class.

I do believe that in my chosen major and minor (criminal justice and sociology, respectively) I have an advantage over some students because of my background. I can identify with many groups and classes of which some students have no practical knowledge. I am glad because I can share different perspectives that may not be obvious to other students.

—Carla

Another Chance to Dance

Since I have just returned to school this semester, the experience of being a nontraditional older student is still very new to me. Actually, this is the second time I have returned to school. More than a decade ago, I went to night school. At the time, I was a struggling single parent, trying to make my way in the workplace. Night classes helped my self-esteem in general and my career in particular. I took all the courses required for my position as a Navy public affairs officer, and although I was extremely pressed for time, I thoroughly enjoyed the school experience.

That was the era of the superwoman and supermom. Being the perfect student and the perfect career woman while raising your children single-handedly was the thing to do. There were many of us "perfect" women in night school, trying to do it all. A lot of us even managed to survive for awhile, but I think we all lost touch with ourselves in the meantime. I know the issue of "doing it all" is still evolving, but I think women have learned a few lessons since the early 1980s. I hope most women feel less need to be perfect these days. During that school experience, I was very much in sync with the cultural standards of the day. My recent return to school has been like that of a thirty-pound-overweight Rockette dancer performing at Radio City Music Hall for a packed audience. It's OK; you were selected for your talent, but everyone just wonders why you're up there!

Today I am a white, middle-class, fifty-two-year-old woman who must devote time both to classes and aging parents. I am the oldest person in each of my three classes, and my problems with my parents are not ones I can share with many of my fellow students. Also, just one year ago, I managed a large Navy public affairs staff. Today, I probably know less than most of my classmates about the material we are currently studying. I went from a powerful position to a powerless one, from supervising young people to being inferior to them in some areas. It can be very disconcerting at times.

Although the students either treat me respectfully or ignore me completely (which is great because I don't want to stand out), I often wonder what they must think of me. Are they saying "Why didn't she go to school earlier?" or "Why should she take up space which a traditional student who still has her career ahead of her might be using?" I also wonder what the professors think. Do I intimidate them by my age? Is it uncomfortable to teach someone older than yourself? Do I participate less in some classes for fear of drawing attention to myself? These are questions I ponder from time to time. However, these thoughts are transitory and most of the time I just feel lucky to have this opportunity to go back to school. I will learn much from the students, and because of my experiences, I believe I have much to contribute.

Most of the time, I shake off my insecurities by telling myself that I have paid my dues and have earned the right to be here. There is no doubt that this experience will greatly enhance the rest of my life and that could be another thirty years or so—plenty of time for a second career. The best part is that I will be operating with the newest educational information, and it will be fresh in my mind—not thirty years old.

When I wonder why I left my job and became a student, I remember that I once dreamed of becoming a writer, and now I have the opportunity to make that dream come true. Then it all makes sense. As an anonymous writer once wrote, "What are we anyway without our dreams?"

—J. S. C.

Will I Ever Be a Writer?

I was born in Iran and am a product of the Iranian educational system. Being a Jew, I learned, even as a child, to brush away the anti-Semitic remarks of the teachers with a smile and to accept the bad grades that came with them with much pride and no protest. However, since I was in an all girls' school, I did not encounter educational sexism until I was in high school, when I had male teachers for the first time. Even now, I don't know which element, the religious or gender bias, has had the most effect in determining the course of my education.

I would have loved to study literature, but my literature teachers were the most anti-Semitic teachers I had. Therefore, I registered as a math major and spent my last two years of high school in a new school with coed classes. I, like my female classmates, graduated from high school a broken person. Studying math mostly with male teachers who favored scientific education for men only and openly discriminated against girls was a traumatic experience.

Losing my enthusiasm for sciences was not as big a sacrifice as giving up writing, the one talent that I could show off in my first high school. My classmates would never leave the classroom unless I had finished reading my essays to them. My teacher, a woman who was not crazy about Jews, often forgot my religious orientation and enthusiastically listened with the rest. In the coed school, the literature teacher was male. Despite protests from the female students, he often interrupted my readings with much annoyance to allow one of the guys to read from his writings.

I don't know how I passed the difficult entrance exam to Pahlavi University. At my father's insistence, I signed up for math again. The first math class I had was with the same teacher who had the habit of humiliating women in high school. By the end of the semester, most women were failing the class. All but one woman changed majors that semester.

I switched to the English department, a move that completely changed my life.

Most of my teachers were American or British. The atmosphere of the department was like that found on a European campus. I excelled in English literature, making straight A's even in Farsi literature with a teacher who did not hide his anti-Semitism. I owe my good grade in the class, however, to my classmates. At one point, when I could not tolerate the teacher's constant screaming at me, I walked out of the class, humiliated and crying. To my surprise, most students, all Moslem, walked out in support of me. The teacher did not try to antagonize me after that.

One of my most influential teachers was a visiting professor from the United States. He encouraged me to continue my education in the United States; that is how I came to ODU for my last year as an undergraduate in English. My first year was a dream. I was doing well, I liked my teachers, and the classmates were wonderful. The most exciting part of the year was my acceptance into the graduate program.

It is funny how I can look back at those years, remembering the joy and the sense of accomplishment I felt. Yet, I realize now that many things were wrong that I could not see at the time. I have to admit that I did not speak very good English. I had a thick Iranian accent that always brought a smile to the face of my teachers—male teachers. I still do not know if the long sessions I had with them in their offices chatting with them were simply a result of their interest in a foreign student or if there was something more there that I was too naive or too overwhelmed by the culture to comprehend. I know the meaning of that smile too well by now. It is a sign of a certain feeling of superiority that I still sense but no longer tolerate. Nothing brings that smile and the twinkle of eyes faster than when I mispronounce a word or do not know its meaning. I am still hesitant in my classes to ask the meaning of a word that is unfamiliar. I often write it down to look it up later at home, even it if means missing part of the interaction in the classroom.

An interesting thing happened one day in my Shakespeare class. Topics were passed around for students to choose for term papers. I put my initials next to the one that I thought was interesting. My teacher refused to allow me to work on the subject. It was too complicated for me, he announced; despite my insistence and the protest of other students, he picked a different topic. I often write about what I don't understand nowadays. I feel that it is a part of the learning process. I have a hard time forgiving myself for allowing him to patronize me.

I stayed in the master's degree program for one year. I knew it was a matter of pride for the department to have a foreign student—a rare occurrence in those days—and that could have been the basis for my acceptance to the program. My acceptance was conditional on taking an English composition course to improve my writing. That was one of the most humiliating experiences I have had. I had been proud of myself for receiving the only A in my Shakespeare class on a term paper. I could not tolerate being in the same class with students fresh out of high school, writing about our favorite recipes. A more advanced class, such as management writing, would have been much more appropriate. I started finding reasons for skipping the class.

Then, one day in the hallways, I heard the head of the department talking to one of my teachers in a rather callous, smirking tone about rapes on campus. One of my classes was at night and I had to depend upon friends to give me a ride home. I had always looked at the United States as a semi-utopia. The same American teacher, who helped me leave Iran, had always painted an idyllic picture of the country for us. Suddenly, culture shock hit. I was feeling alienated, disillusioned, and lost. I was paralyzed with fear and unhappy in my progress. I finished that year with an incomplete in the writing class, a C in my night class, and B's for the rest. I had lost a certain sense of purpose. I left school that year to marry and did not return for fifteen years.

During those years, I worked, had three children, and drowned myself in volunteering. The need for writing, however, never disappeared. One day, my sister came to a family gathering and showed me a large notebook she had saved for many years. She had been allowed to take only a small bag out of Iran when she emigrated, but she had chosen to pack some of my writings. I was shocked to see all those who could read

Farsi hovering around the writings for hours. I decided then it was time for me to go back to school.

I wanted very much to take a class in creative writing, but the class was full. Instead, I decided out of simple curiosity to enroll in women's studies through the Institute of Humanities. This has been a unique experience for me.

At times, I have felt that it is a personal goal of my teachers in the graduate program to help me succeed. I have learned to analyze, whereas most of my previous training had been to memorize. Most classes I have taken towards my M.A. have been literature courses. For the first time, I was able to identify with most novels I was reading. Most importantly, I have been encouraged to explore my culture and to think more seriously about writing.

It has been refreshing to be in classes in which an accent is okay. The multicultural atmosphere in the humanities and women's studies classes has given me a more comfortable environment to express myself, because I am not the only one who speaks "funny."

Will I ever be a writer? I am writing a paper on the effect of education on women writers of the developing world. Most non-western novelists who write in English had knowledge of Western culture and English language as children. The odds are against me. However well I can write English, I can write amazingly better and much faster in Farsi, although I rarely use the language. I have started writing some short stories about life in a Jewish ghetto in Iran. Although they may not be in beautiful English, they will chronicle a life little known outside a small, vanishing group of people.

It is with a great sense of sadness that I am leaving school this year. I am finally graduating from the M.A. program this semester. A few days ago, I met one of my teachers I had not seen for a long time. "You should write," she said. I told her I was. I only wished I had had teachers like her a bit earlier.

—Alyssa Rubin

Typical All-American Boy

I often view myself as the typical all-American boy. I was raised in an upper-middle-class family with both parents at home. Church is a weekly crusade, we eat three planned meals a day, and we have a strong sense of family traditions. Growing up, I was taught by my family to balance being honest, respectful, and caring with being logical, proud, and stern. My parents also taught me the value of education and the benefits that can be reaped from it. My family is known in my city as my dad is a local politician, and I soon learned that more was expected of me because of my family. I was constantly reminded, not only by my parents but also by my teachers, of how I was to act and perform in school.

The junior high school that I went to was a school with an excellent academic reputation. The majority of the students were white at this school, but the social classes differed quite a bit. After the first year there (seventh grade), the classes began to get more concentrated and the students began to be the same in each class. It seemed as if some of us were "picked from the crop,"and we were expected to perform better than our counterparts in other classes. What I am sure is not coincidental is that we all had the same story: middle- to upper-middle-class, two-parent homes, older brothers or sisters who did well in school, and white. We all got to know each other at an early age and we grew up together in and out of the classroom. The friendships and support that we gained from one another were vital in our maturing academically and socially.

Going from my junior high school to a high school that was seventy percent black was like going to a new world, and it took quite an adjustment. There were two other junior high schools (predominantly black) that fed into my high school, but most of the students in the honor classes were still the same. The new "members" were not all white, but they were in the same economic class and had the same type of family life.

Once we all settled into our places among the academic elite at my school, we began to notice that we often received special treatment from guidance counselors, vice principals, and even the principal. We could get away with the little things that other students would get detention for, and we often took advantage of those situations. Another example of the special treatment was how interested our teachers were in us as individuals. They often wanted to see us after school for "help sessions," although they usually engaged us in simple chat and advice on life rather than offering help.

The experience that I found on the university campus was much different than the one I had in high school. Now, at a school that was ninety percent white, I felt as if the whole university was against me. The professors rarely used my name, and some of them did not even know it to use it if they wanted to. They did not care if I showed up for class, and they seemed uninterested in whether I made an A or a D on a test. I often would go through a whole semester not speaking in class nor talking with the professor after class. I was content to just sit in the middle of the classroom, taking the notes, and not caring if the professor knew who I was or not.

I knew that I had the ability to perform, but it took about one semester to get used to the new system that I was working under. There was no longer any pressure applied from my professors, advisors, or the competition from my friends. Nobody at my university knew who I was and could probably care less if I told them. I began to like it this way. I found my grades improved, and I actually enjoyed being that anonymous student who received an A.

Now in my senior year of college, I believe that I have learned more than the average student in terms of usable knowledge. I know that I received some extra care along the way, but I also believe that in certain ways I was discriminated against. It is unfair to pick students out because they look smart or come from that certain family. I also think it is unfair to have huge expectations of such students. These expectations place a pressure on them to perform for the school, the teachers, and the parents, rather than for themselves. Many of my friends never did adjust to the university's way of looking at students equally and are now dubbed "underachievers" since they dropped out or did not make the expected grades. I am glad that I realized what the system was all about, but I am disturbed at how unfairly it works. I am sure many capable students who were overlooked in my school district may now be considered overachievers as they have beaten the system, but there needs to be a change in the way all students go through the turnstiles of academia.

—Wabbit

On Guard Before I Speak

I don't feel that I was ever pigeonholed as a freshman at ODU, but since I was a white male with a high school education, I believe that it was understood that I would pursue higher education. Counselors always assumed that because I was white and from a middle-class family, I would go to college. I played football with students who did not get the same kind of treatment I did because of their race and economic position. They were "diverted" to pursue "their place in life." It all seemed so unremarkable at the time, but it happened to me, too.

Once at the university, I, too, became a victim. I was denied financial assistance because I had been brought up with two full sets of parents with successful careers. Many of my peers were allowed grants, loans, and even scholarships because they grew up in standard two-parent families. The financial aid forms never asked my father and stepmother how much money my mother and stepfather were contributing to my education. It was just assumed that there would be lots of money for me because both of my parents were remarried to other young urban professionals.

In class, it was taboo to discuss religions as viable agents of cause or effect. In criminal justice classes, I have felt as though I were "the bad guy" because of my race. Whites are now asked to take the blame for all the past, present, and future ills of the world. White males, who for centuries have been authorities on the subjects of crimes against all people, are now discredited and accused of being biased against women and blacks.

The present climate within our educational institution is very stagnant and politically correct. This offends my intelligence, to be quite honest. When I take classes titled Violence Against Women or Juvenile Delinquency with female or black instructors, I should not have to be constantly on guard when

I speak out. And this problem is not exclusive to me or to those particular classes. I see people in my classes, many of whom do not even fit the profile of a traditional college-age white male student, who are also afraid to join in the discussion for fear of being persecuted.

We are all so afraid of offending someone else that it keeps the truth from surfacing. Things that should be discussed are not mentioned. Things that should be kept to one's self are a part of the public discussion. I wonder how these things will affect my children's children when they have to deal with a society like ours.

—Christopher

I've Learned to Fight Racial Hatred

In my three and a half years at this university, I have heard and witnessed a lot of things, some good and some bad. There are times when I ask myself why I went here instead of a predominantly black college. Then I think back to all the friendships I've built and the good times I have enjoyed, and the memories erase all the doubts that I have.

In high school, I took college preparatory classes so that I would know what to expect when I got to college. My classes usually had no more than four black students out of a class of thirty-five. I'm from a middle-class family, so it was fairly easy for me to blend in with my classmates. When I came to Old Dominion, I somehow thought things might be different. I thought that there would be more black students in my classes, but to my surprise there weren't. Three years later, the number of white students in my classes is almost double the number of blacks. I thought by now something would have changed but obviously nothing has.

My first bad experience at this school happened when I was a freshman living in one of the dormitories. One of my friends had a white roommate and they really didn't get along that well. At first, my friend thought her roommate was a bit antisocial, but as the year moved on, I could tell it went a little deeper than that. When I visited my friend, her roommate would never speak to us. She would sit on her bed and read without acknowledging that either of us was in the room. She even went as far as to put a curtain around her bed so she could isolate herself from us whenever we were in the room. I think I finally let myself realize what was going on when she and Andrea got into a heated argument. One day the room-mate finally let her true feelings out. She told my friend that she was a "no-good nigger" and that she would not allow herself to live any longer with the likes of her kind.

I couldn't believe what I was hearing. I knew that racism still existed, but somehow I had let myself believe that it was the older generations that still carried this hatred around. The hatred in her words truly scared me, but I think that maybe her saying this did me a favor. It brought me out of the protected world my parents had kept me in for eighteen years. It made me realize that the world is still far from being free of hate, and it is close to slipping back into an era that was filled with violence and hatred for one another every day.

I'm sad to say that this is not the only incident of racism I have witnessed at Old Dominion. A few years ago, I heard a group of white students talking in the lounge area of the student center about the ineffective performance by Virginia's governor, who was then Douglas Wilder. The students must not have realized I was sitting there because one stated, "That's what Virginia gets for electing a black man into office." Someone must have noticed me listening because they nudged the guy and he looked at me and blushed, obviously embarrassed that I had heard his outburst.

I haven't let these bad experiences keep me from getting to know white students. In fact, I roomed with two white girls my sophomore year and I consider them to be two of my best friends. These negative experiences have made me a stronger person. I've learned the only way to fight racial hatred is to ignore it and to gain as much knowledge as I can. I hope that I can help in eliminating this hatred so that the next generation doesn't have to endure it as I and my ancestors have had to.

Since I've been taking classes at Old Dominion, I've never had a professor treat me unfairly because of my sex or race. I have been disappointed by some of my professors' lack of focus on blacks and their role in history. In the American history class that I took, my professor spoke of blacks briefly and insignificantly. I was really upset by his lack of interest and lack of respect for my culture. I am glad to say that my second semester history teacher made an effort to inform and enlighten the class about the achievements and contributions of blacks throughout history.

Last year, I had an African-American professor for a criminal justice class. I was glad to see a black female professor teaching at the university because finally I had a teacher to whom I could truly relate. The only thing that upset me was the lack of respect that other students in the class gave her. I hope that I'm not sounding like I'm singling out just whites, but in this class, there was a group of males who were truly disrespectful of the professor. Anytime she tried to broaden our views on blacks and the misconceptions about blacks and crime, they began to talk loudly and make disruptive noises. Many times, she had to reprimand these students for disturbing her lecture. A couple of other students of different races and I heard them make racist remarks, but fortunately for them and all of us no altercations took place.

I must say that despite all the bad experiences that I have had, I still remain open to the thoughts and opinions of other students. One day, I'm going to be a lawyer and to do that I will have to be able to relate to all races and cultures. My ambition has not always been to be a lawyer. When I first came to this university, my advisor steered me towards nursing courses and an education major. I guess she thought that since I was a girl, I wanted to do something nurturing. I don't know why she didn't ask me if I was interested in biology or engineering. Maybe she thought those majors were out of my league, but I personally don't believe that they were. I am almost ready to graduate and I'm proud to say I think I'm going to do exceptionally well in my field. The experiences that I have gained at Old Dominion have helped me grow as a person. In class, I try to make other people more aware of my culture and our struggles as a people by participating in discussions. I think the only way to fight ignorance is by informing people and dispelling their misconceptions about African-American people.

—F. B.

To Succeed as a Woman

Being a graduate student at Old Dominion University is a struggle. My educational background and my gender are constant reminders of my "place" at the university.

My parents immigrated from Europe in order to have a better life and succeeded in entering the middle class. They were idealistic about American public school, believing my siblings and I would be better off culturally in an inner-city school environment where we would experience the American melting pot.

My high school experience was beneficial in some aspects and a disappointment in others. I was in a diverse cultural environment that enabled me to mix pleasurably with people of all colors and religions. Although I am of Italian and Scottish ancestry, most of my closest friends are Latino, and I learned to speak Spanish in the hallways of my high school. This inner-city school, on the other hand, lacked the necessary ingredients to prepare me for college study. Most of the teachers, too busy disciplining their classes, were unable to teach. They were frustrated with the students, believing them to be incapable of handling challenging work. We were forced to do "busy work," and I grew accustomed to this method of pedagogy.

Looking back, I feel my race was an advantage in school. Being white gave me access to honors classes, better teachers, and newer textbooks. My race and class ultimately gave me one advantage that many of my Latino and African-American friends would never have: an opportunity to go to college. College was a requirement in my family, despite my lackluster performance in high school. I entered a pre-veterinary program in Pennsylvania, and this was the beginning of my struggle. I remember sitting in my freshman biology class, waiting for my midterm exam to be handed back to me. The professor humiliated me by commenting, "It's a good thing you have your looks, honey—you can marry a vet instead of becoming one." This was the first, but not the last, example of gender bias with which I would be faced. After this experience, I quit college and decided never to return. I felt like a failure in the classroom. I also lost confidence in myself as a woman; maybe I was just buying the idea that women and medicine don't mix.

My parents made such a fuss about my going back to school that I took some classes at a community college. There, I got a second chance and found teachers who were able to teach instead of discourage. At Brookdale Community College, teachers were more concerned about students learning than about assigning grades. Brookdale had only three grades: credit, credit with honors, and credit with high honors. Everyone had the opportunity to earn credit with high honors by retaking tests, rewriting papers, and doing extra assignments. Finally, I could focus on learning instead of worrying about my grades.

Many teachers there showed interest in my studies and encouraged me to keep learning and persevere. I found out how much I enjoyed reading after I took my first literature class. One professor really inspired me to work hard. She kept telling me how important it was for me to succeed as a woman. I didn't know what she meant at the time, but I understand completely now. She and other teachers gave me the encouragement I needed to finish the program. After I graduated with an A.A. degree in social science, I continued part-time at Kean College in Union City, New Jersey. I also felt at home at that school, where many people like me were trying to survive. Race and gender did not seem to play a part in the classroom or the university setting.

With my B.S. in management science, I began working in marketing for a major liquor company. The company paid extremely well, and my managers were impressed with my work. But I saw rampant gender bias, and after watching a pregnant woman drinking vodka with a straw at one of my inner-city accounts, I decided that I was not going to waste my life promoting a product that destroys people.

In my search for equality, I figured I would challenge myself with more education. I thought getting away from business would save me from gender bias; however, once again I have been reminded about my "place" by a male faculty member at this institution. He has advised me that women are supposed to "play the game" in order to make it through graduate school, instead of simply learning the material like male students. When I resisted his assessment of my capabilities, he reminded me that he was the Ph.D. and made vague threats about his power to thwart the successful completion of my graduate program.

Where do I run to now for equality? There is nowhere to go. I would much rather struggle to succeed intellectually than to combat gender bias in the classroom. I ask myself constantly why I keep going. The answer is that I have a passion for learning. I also know that my case is not the worst scenario. There are many women in this world struggling not only with the gender issue, but with race and class issues as well. Women like Rigoberta Menchú, a Nobel Peace Prize winner from Guatemala, have inspired me to fight for equality in both race and gender.

When I enter classrooms here at ODU, I bring with me my experiences with Latin-American culture. I want to be the voice that encourages discussion about the importance of intercultural respect. My love for the Latin culture stems back to my high school days and the vacations I spent in Puerto Rico with my best friend's family. My travels through Central America, especially Honduras, have focused my goals in life. I have witnessed women being treated as mules without any rights in their own land. I want to combine my interests in helping women with my passion for Hispanic culture. The gender issue is something I am forced to combat in order to survive in a patriarchal environment. Academia will never let me forget my gender.

I have learned many things in the classroom, but I also obtained knowledge in the hallways of high school, the cafeterias of the business world, and the offices of university faculty. These are the places in which I was reminded where my place was "supposed" to be and what games I "had" to play. While the recent experiences with the professor shook me and gave me a moment's doubt about myself, they did not drive me from the classroom as that incident in my freshman year did. In many ways, these experiences have made me tough, but they do not change the person I am inside. I will not play the "female bimbo" role that many people in both business and academia would prefer for me, for I am strong, not just as a woman, but as a human being.

I am determined to graduate successfully from this program via hard work and perseverance, the way any other student would expect to earn a degree. I will not tolerate idle threats from professors or accept game-playing as an appropriate way of pursuing my education or as a way in which to live my life. It is only now that I understand what my mentor at Brookdale Community College was saying to me: "To succeed as a woman . . ." I also keep pursuing education because I think about the struggle of the women in Honduras. Many of them will never have the opportunity to study and ultimately to make change. I do not feel powerful at ODU, but I do not feel powerless. I am optimistic about the future. I am older and wiser now; no one, not even a Ph.D., is going to discourage me about my future.

—K. D.

Not Your Typical Student

I believe that in many ways I am not your typical student—and for that I am thankful, as my experiences have left me more receptive and open-minded than many people I meet. I am also very appreciative for the opportunity to attend school and to do something worthwhile with my life.

I am a "thirty-something" divorced mother of two, a recovering alcoholic, and a lesbian. Because of these different experiences, I find that I am sometimes impatient with students who aren't taking their lives or their studies seriously. I truly envy these kids their opportunity to get through school at a much younger age than I will.

When I graduated from high school, I had the opportunity to get a scholarship. My parents, however, were dead set against my going on to college. Much of their opposition was a result of the influence of their religious beliefs, which strongly discouraged higher education as a waste of time. I have always regretted that I didn't stand up to my parents. On the other hand, our religion encouraged a great deal of learning and reading on an individual level as well as writing and researching topics in great depth. We were also taught how to express ourselves and how to become public speakers. From that perspective, I've always felt that I had an advantage over many other students.

My religious upbringing also left me with a great deal of guilt about my lesbianism. At first, I was filled with a lot of shame and believed that I didn't deserve to have anything good happen to me. I've come a long way since then. Here in school, I exercise caution in coming out, though I'm out at work and to some of my family. It isn't because of being ashamed; I've protested at the Christian Broadcasting Network in Virginia Beach and I marched on Washington one April with a million other gays. (Yes, there were a million of us there!) And in class, I will defend gay rights and state my views. But I am neither willing nor prepared to deal with homophobic professors and students. I'm studying to work with children, and in Virginia I can't be a lesbian and work with kids. Sometimes I find that I am hurt by the ignorant and cruel comments people make. Yet, healing always occurs when I encounter an open-minded person. I firmly believe that good education will help end the prejudice one day.

A problem that I have only recently faced is my alcoholism. I have been alcohol and drug free for almost three years. It was after my first anniversary of being sober that I decided it was time to take responsibility for my life and do something that would validate me as an individual. That was when I applied to school.

So, how have all of these things affected my attitude in the classroom? I sometimes feel like an outsider, as if I don't belong or fit in. This makes it difficult to make any close friends, which is something that I miss. It is very important to me to do well—not just well, but extremely well. This attitude isn't always fair to myself, as it sets up unreasonable expectations and fails to take into account that I am human. By the same token, however, I am getting my money's worth out of every class. I'm willing to take risks and express myself, even when I know other people will think I'm foolish or will disagree with me. I'm also not too concerned with winning any popularity contests, so I have the freedom to be myself.

The decision to return to school was a scary one, but it is one which I have never regretted. I love the feeling of growth and of being challenged to succeed. My life has a purpose it never had before. Sometimes it is frustrating trying to take care of all my responsibilities—but I wouldn't trade this for the world.

—D. B.

The University Is a Tool

As an older student starting college at the age of twenty-six, I have found that in many classroom situations, age has a positive influence on how younger classmates perceive me. There may be several reasons for this. Being older, I am somewhat more responsible than my younger classmates. I am also more cautious in speaking out—if I have a question, I will wait instead of disrupting class. If I do ask a question, I make sure it is an intelligent one. This has led to others viewing me as a much better student than I believe I am.

Age is probably the only factor that separates me from being just another face in the scholastic crowd. I am a white male with no disabilities, who fits right into the typical WASP model. Since I was raised on a number of air force bases around the country and in Europe, I have no accent or regional affiliation. My family could be considered well off both in monetary terms and in reading, writing, and discussing ideas. As a child, I was exposed to a fairly broad cross-section of society, and I am comfortable in a variety of situations. As I am a mechanical engineering major, being a male has been an asset. I had many technical experiences in my childhood which have broadened my outlook on the way things work. My hobbies consist of railway history and the building of outdoor railway trains. This I consider to be an asset to my engineering studies, since I spend a lot of time designing mechanisms and building cars and structures.

I do not feel that I have been discriminated against in any way while at Old Dominion University. I have not really noticed any discrimination directed at others. There have been instances where a female in an engineering class has asked a silly question and there have been a number of smiles passed around, but the same happens to male students so this is probably not discrimination. I have seen derogatory posters and bathroom scribbles of an antigay nature. There was an instance in the Arts and Letters building where the instructor closed the classroom door, and the back of the door had a rather large poster affixed to it. The poster had a picture of a man performing fellatio on another man with a distasteful antigay message. If I had been gay, I definitely would have felt intimidated.

If I had chosen another major, I might feel differently about how I'm perceived in class. I really can't see myself as a liberal arts or education major. My wife says that I am too serious, and I am to the extent that I don't like frivolous or irrelevant classes. I resent having to take a philosophy class. I am a well-rounded person and dislike the university imposing certain requirements in order to "make me a better person."

I cannot say that I feel that I belong at this university. The university is a tool that one uses to further their career. In engineering, students have little extra time for social functions and clubs. The few groups I do belong to are professional organizations that I intend to use to further my career.

—Peter

Keeping My Focus

I am a thirty-year-old female student from a lower-middle-class family of six children. We are of Irish, English, and Mexican descent. My family did not starve, but we never seemed to have much money either. The focus of our home was on my father's needs first and then on the activities and hobbies of my four brothers. My mother's needs never seemed to be considered. She was the last to be served a meal and the last to get a new pair of shoes. My sisters and I fell somewhere in between. I learned early that the focus of my life was to attend to the needs and desires of others. I have also obtained a high level of tolerance for discomfort.

A college education was not discussed as a possibility for my siblings or me. This may be because there was not enough money to send six children to college, or it may be because an education was not seen as necessary for a successful life and it was assumed that my belief and trust in God would be sufficient for all my needs. I graduated from high school thinking myself too "dumb" to attempt college. I know that this was due to a lack of organization, self-confidence, and good study habits, for which I fault my parents as well as the school system. I turned to the military as an alternative and entered the Marine Corps at the age of eighteen. I graduated from boot camp ranked number two in my platoon, which should have been my first clue that I was not as dumb as I thought I was. I didn't catch on.

After being discharged at the end of my contract, I was frustrated by my inability to obtain jobs I was interested in because I lacked a college education. I had to work full time and go to school part time. This increased the number of years it took to achieve my goal. This frustration and the realization (in a psychology class) that my IQ was not one of a "dumb" person, as well as the determination to succeed, have led me to attend school full time and to work full time as well. I don't have time for friends, family, my dog, and many times even my husband right now. Small responsibilities such as shopping for groceries, cleaning house, and car repairs have become major obstacles and annoyances. I am always rushed. It is difficult to explore topics that interest me because my free time is so limited. As a commuter, I don't get to know other students or professors very well because I don't have time before or after class to stop and talk; I am rushing back to work. As a result of this, as well as my age, I feel detached from the general student population.

I do feel that my age and past experience make me a more focused student. Since I come from a home where children were to be seen and not heard (and if you were female, it did not matter if you were a child or not), I have difficulty speaking up in class. I am currently in my third year of school, and I am just beginning to force myself to join in class discussions. My desire for an education has also coincided with a time in my life when I felt I needed to decide whether or not I wanted to have children. I have lost four pregnancies in the last two years, further complicating this endeavor. I am torn between the proverbial "biological clock" and pursuance of my goals.

I find that my European ancestry is very well represented in the classroom but that Mexican-American history is practically nonexistent. I am often confronted with very different views from the conservative Baptist ones that I was raised with. I feel that all the information available is not presented, so students are not given the option of forming their own opinions. I am offended by the presentation of material as "fact" when it is often opinion or conjecture on the part of the individual or the institution. I have tried to consider all the information presented in the classroom, have kept what I felt was relevant to me, and have discarded that which wasn't. I think my age and past experience have helped me to do this as well.

My choice of study has been greatly influenced by my upbringing. I am drawn to caretaking positions which involve children rather than those that require high levels of competition. It is my desire to teach children in grades four through eight. I feel this is the time in children's lives to instill in them the skills they will need to succeed in school and life. It is also an important time in the development of their confidence. I hope to prevent someone else from delaying or abandoning their dreams. I continue to receive negative feedback from my employer, "friends," and my family about my decision to pursue a degree at this time in my life. It has taken me a long time to learn that the most important opinions in my life are first those of God and second those which I hold of myself. This keeps me focused.

—I. E. S.

Color Me Orange

Old Dominion University classifies me, a returning student, as "nontraditional." That classification is on target. I do not fit neatly into the model of the traditional undergraduate student: single, eighteen to twenty-two years old with some dependence on parents for financial support. In the classroom, I am nontraditional as well. My motivation is different. I am not in school to get ahead. I'm in school to catch up.

My age is sometimes a handicap. Professors look at me and comment to the class, "Those of you who already think they know everything will not do well in my class!" Think I know everything! Each day I realize how much I *don't* know about anything, including myself. Age does not automatically equate to omniscience. In several of my classes, I have been older than the professors. This makes me ill at ease, and I wonder if they feel threatened by my seniority in years. Perhaps it is my own paranoia, knowing that I have so much catching up to do. No matter. I fiercely trudge ahead, trying to close the gap between years and knowledge. I will catch up, with or without the soothing unguent of the professors' encouraging nods. I will unravel the mysteries of geometry. I will learn the fauna and flora of the Ordovician period.

"Are you just auditing this class, or are you taking it for credit?" the students ask. I'm taking it for credit, and my life's experiences don't earn me extra points. Education is different these days. I went to school in the "memorize and regurgitate" era. Now the style of education stresses thinking, integration of facts, and the application of these facts to specific situations. Even grammar has changed. Now there are HP4's and PoD's (post determiners). And passive verbs now can have direct objects on occasion. What happened to nouns "functioning" as adjectives?

My previous learning experiences make me feel most comfortable in the large lecture halls. I know the drill. Take notes, learn the dates, and memorize the succession of kings. I can match and fill in the blanks, but choosing the *best* answer from five equally confusing statements which require me to apply facts to a given situation leaves my heart racing and my palms sweaty. (When in doubt, choose "B"—or is it "C"?) Imagine it; since I was in school, Columbus didn't discover America. The play I wrote in seventh grade is no longer historically correct. Little did I know that one day Columbus would be described as the scourge of the hemisphere and murderer of men.

I am pleased with the new courses I have discovered relating to the contributions of women and blacks. Classes in the history of Latin America or the dynasties in Japan are not only worthwhile, they are necessary also. It is imperative that we discover women's true role in war and in peace and that we all have a greater understanding of the history of African Americans. However, since this "truth in history" concept is new to me, I feel I have a great deal of catching up to do.

Growing up with two perfectionist parents who strictly adhered to the "Every Tub Stands on His Own Bottom" and

"Little Red Hen" theories has made me very independent. I carry this independence into the classroom. I was admonished that studying with someone was a complete waste of time. The thought for the day in our home was, "You can do anything if you want to and if you work hard enough." I rarely admit to myself that I cannot master a concept. My mouth does not form the words, "I can't," because "can't" was not allowed in my vocabulary. However, I am learning to adapt new ways to the old rules. I am learning, although sometimes very slowly, to ask for help and to study in groups. I bow to the need for a math tutor. For me, the tutor is more essential than the textbook. I want to do well in math, and I certainly try hard enough, but the mere thought of a parabola or an equilateral triangle evokes the tortures of hell in my brain. Girls, except me, were not necessarily expected to do well in math subjects. I did my best (and only an A was acceptable best in my parents' eyes!) in the subjects in which girls were supposed to excel. I had pretty handwriting. I read above grade level. I learned to cook and sew in home economics. But I got a C in geometry. My parents insisted that I drop the class. Today, I admit that I am frightened to take the required university math courses. But that fighter spirit rears in my soul, and I say to myself, "I WILL SURVIVE IT!" Part of my education is learning how to accept that my best does not always equate to an A.

I chose ODU because the program of my choice was here. Neither the color nor the gender of the professors and the majority of the students is of consequence to me. Quality of education is. I have dropped classes at ODU because I had poor instructors. There are those labels: "male chauvinist" and "feminist." I am neither. Perhaps I should create another category and call myself a "neuterist." Quality teaching is quality teaching, and shoddy work is shoddy work, whether the professor (or the student) is black, white, red, yellow, male, female, or a combination of all of the above. I have learned to look beyond the superficial exterior of people. Dedication and effectiveness are the qualities I look for. I believe quality work transcends race and gender. I believe in equal opportunity. I live it in my everyday life. Because I tend to look for the good in people, I usually find it. The good that I look for is inherent in all races. My romantic view of life has not failed me at Old Dominion University. I do not reserve goodness for Caucasians or men.

However, I can find none of that goodness in silence after a professor asks a question. My participation in a discussion class is painful but not nearly so painful to me as that silence. I much prefer to sit and listen, harking back to the "seen and not heard" days of my childhood, I suppose; but the continuing silence unnerves me. "Won't somebody please say something?" I think to myself. Then I blurt out some statement designed to break that uncomfortable spell. I may try to answer reasonably, or I may try to play the devil's advocate. Although I do not necessarily relish all eyes on me, I'll take the chance that my answer will start the discussion. I'm not afraid to be wrong, but I am afraid of the silence. Because someone else will have to fill this deafening void when I graduate, I have begun a training program. I occasionally say nothing when a professor asks a question and no one has a ready answer. The professors become impatient and rephrase the question. I make myself look down. I must keep quiet. Someone else will have to take a chance. Someone else will have to be The Good Hands.

Finishing college will give me the chance to fulfill my career goal of many years ago: to teach. Teaching has been my goal since I was a child. Perhaps it is my need to fulfill the nurturing role. I see teaching as sharing what I love: to learn. Returning to school is both a luxury and a necessity for me. When I left college after my freshman year to get married, I soon learned that I would never be happy without my degree. I promised my parents and myself that I would graduate from college some day. It has been a promise I have not broken and a goal I have not given up for thirty years.

"And just who do you think will hire you, old as you are?" my mother asks.

"With all your education you're going to be so smart you won't be able to talk to us," my sister buzzes, stinging as painfully as a bumblebee.

If I were to paint a real portrait of myself in the classroom, the eyes must reflect the pain of these remarks. I must find a steely gray to paint the strong backbone of determination to succeed welded into my soul by all of those Benjamin Franklin-like axioms drilled into me as a child. I would have neither predominantly male nor female features. The style of the painting must be realism. I know my strengths and weaknesses. Perhaps my aversion to math is genetic, or perhaps it is the result of the male domination of those classes in the schools of yesterday. I must hold English and history books in my hands—they are my strong suits. I would disregard the realism long enough to paint my skin orange. It is a color of vibrancy and vitality equal to the elation I feel knowing that I can still compete with the younger students. I'd paint the wrinkles around my eyes as a reminder that I consider education a serious quest. But the mouth must be smiling with a slight smirk. I'm going for the gusto. And, yes, I know that I am selfish. This education is for me.

—Doris Lowe

5

Conclusion

These essays have aided us both as students and teachers. As students, we learned things from our peers that helped us to understand our own responses to the classroom as well as those of the student seated next to us in class. As teachers, we have learned about how our own demeanor in the classroom is interpreted differently by different students. We have learned also about our students, perhaps especially about the silent among them; those who give us little clue as to what engages their interest or violates their deepest sense of the world.

Some of what we learned from the essays reinforces the literature on multiculturalism in education. We see, for instance, that both students' and teachers' expectations play a significant role in students' accomplishments and sense of self-confidence. Older students believe that they demand more of themselves than do younger students and feel that their life experience and their active choice to attend a university, often at economic sacrifice, contribute to their success. Similarly, international students who have come to the United States for educational opportunities not available in their home countries expect to have to work hard and to do well. The African-American student essayists are committed to making the most of their educations; their belief that they can accomplish whatever they set their minds to is balanced by an awareness that the world will judge them by more stringent standards than it does others.

The few graduate student teaching assistants who contributed essays were especially clear on the importance of teachers' assumptions about students, for they were simultaneously experiencing the university as students and as apprentice teachers. Young women and minority students write of experiencing condescension more often than do white male or older female students, who worry instead that too much is expected of them. The gratification expressed by those students who experienced real encouragement by faculty members is marked. Sometimes it seems that student demands are very modest. The mere act of being urged by professors to ask questions, even potentially "stupid" ones, is seen as a novelty and a morale builder. That female essayists were more likely to mention the significance of positive reinforcement they have received at Old Dominion University may reflect earlier experiences of relative indifference on the part of teachers to their intellectual development; research confirms this. While women's studies faculty certainly are not the only teachers who go out of their way to help students, the emphasis in feminist pedagogy on taking women students seriously and on paying respect to student voices possibly makes those faculty members teaching women's studies courses more consistently attentive to students than faculty in other disciplines. This, in addition to course content, may explain why so many female students single out women's studies classes as a turning point in their academic lives.

Our collection of essays is inherently biased toward those students who—at least to the point of writing these essays—have survived the university educational system. In interpreting their writing, we consequently were more attuned to what has contributed to their survival than we were to signs of their discouragement or failure. Not all ODU students, even conscientious ones, receive encouragement from their instructors, and the essays reveal some of their efforts to deal with lack of affirmation. Those who stick it out seem to be able to find some means of providing themselves with the encouragement they need, whether it be from peers in the classroom or residence halls or from family, or from a sense of purpose or direction that transcends what happens in any given course.

Many of these students are the first in their families to attend a university. The world of the college campus is a new one for them, and its strangeness extends beyond unfamiliarity with course requirements. Whatever their reason for having chosen this school, once they arrive at Old Dominion, the real work of bridging the gap between their culture of origin and the university falls to them. This is a topic on which the student essayists speak with muted voices. Some students wish to see themselves reflected in their courses, hence their mention of women's studies, courses on African Americans, introduction of materials about gay and lesbian life, and of the relative absence of Hispanic culture and history in the classroom. For the most part, the students seem to assume that the process of adjustment is theirs to make. If they are self-conscious about coming from a working-class background or about doing better with one style of teaching than another, these are personal concerns without any political agenda attached to them.

The response of many students to the university is silence. Clearly, this does not apply to all; the essayist who was originally from India finds that American students have much greater verbal skills than he was accustomed to finding among his peers. Nonetheless, this collection throws light on the kinds of silence that emanate from students' cultural backgrounds. Some international students have language difficulties or are self-conscious about their accents. One working-class American student acknowledges frankly that her limited vocabulary kept her from participating in class or from going to see professors during office hours. Other students wish to avoid being designated as a racial spokesperson, and still others suspect that their appearance leads their professors to require proof of intelligence before they will be encouraged to speak. Some women students are accustomed to giving precedence to male students or feel their contributions to be undervalued by the professor or are fearful of dominating classroom discussion. And, for some students, silence is a form of protest, signaling their resistance, initial or complete, to their required presence in a course on women or minorities or something else designed to "enlighten" them.

Gone are the days when university communities were homogeneous enough to pretend that there were no differences among college students and professors. We will not understand our universities as they are today unless we listen to the voices of the students who now fill the seats in the classrooms. *Ourselves as Students: Multicultural Voices in the Classroom* enables us to hear those voices for the first time.

Appendix A

Appendix B

Bibliography

Appendix A

Table A.1. Old Dominion University Student Body
(Undergraduate and Graduate)

Total undergraduate and graduate student body	15,974
Part-time students	27%
Average age of undergraduates	24 years
Average age of freshmen	20 years
Average age of seniors	27 years
Average age of graduate students	34 years
Graduate students as percentage of student body	32%
Female students as percentage of student body	51%
In-state students	83%
In-region students	63%
International students	4%
Countries represented	86
Students who live in campus residence halls or within neighborhood zip code	21%
On-campus (as opposed to satellite centers) classroom attendance	87%
Distribution of freshman students by ethnic group	
White	64%
African American	17%
Hispanic	2%
Asian and Pacific Islander	9%
Native American	1%
Other	7%

Source: Old Dominion University Office of University Planning and Institutional Research.

Note: These statistics are based on the 1993–94 academic year during which most of the essays in this volume were written.

Table A.2. Old Dominion University Faculty

University faculty	626
Women faculty	27%
Men faculty	73%

Distribution of women faculty across the university

	% of faculty in each college who are women	% of ODU women faculty who are in this college
Arts and Letters	41	39
Business and Public Administration	21	12
Education	36	18
Engineering and Technology	5	2
Health Sciences	75	18
Sciences	11	10

Distribution of faculty by ethnic group	% of ODU faculty
White	83.7%
African American	6.4
Hispanic	0.9
Asian and Pacific Islander	8.6
Native American	0.3

Source: Old Dominion University Office of University Planning and Institutional Research.

Appendix B

The following are a project description and a release form that were given to the fifty-eight students whose essays appear in this book.

Portrait of Yourself as a Student

Do gender, race, social class, religion, nationality, age, sexual orientation, and physical disability get left at the classroom door so that we all enter the classroom simply as "students" or do we bring these other identities with us into the classroom?

In 2–4 typed pages, provide a sociological analysis of yourself as a student in the university classroom in terms of your gender, race, and social class. Add any other variable that you feel applies to you. The following is a list of questions that you do not need to answer systematically, but which may help you think about a topic that you may not have thought about before.

Are there certain subjects that you were drawn to as major fields of study because of your race, gender, and social class, or contrarily, certain subjects that you feel were closed off to you because of these very same factors? Are you, as a member of these various categories, reflected in what is taught in your courses? Do they affect how you are treated by your instructors and fellow students? Do these identities have an impact on what you are open to hearing in class and what you are resistant to? Do they have anything to do with why you are talkative or silent in class or why you have an easier time with some course materials than others? Do you feel as if you "belong" at this university? In what ways has your class background prepared you or not prepared you for university life?

Think not only of the aspects of gender, race, and class that might make you uncomfortable in any given classroom or in the university, but also of those parts of your identity that might enhance your sense of belonging. For instance, imagine what it would be like to be someone of "another" group in some of your classes, e.g. a female in an engineering class or the only African American in your sociology class or a lesbian or gay student in a course on marriage and family or a deaf student in any class, and then reflect on what you take for granted in your ordinary classroom experience.

Release Form

I, _____ *(please print)* of

Local Address   *Permanent Address*

_____   _____

_____   _____

_____   _____

Tel. no. _____   Tel. no. _____

release my interest in and ownership of my "portrait of myself as a student" essay to Dr. Anita Clair Fellman (and an editorial collective) for possible use in a published collection of student self-portraits. I understand that I will not receive any monetary compensation for my essay.

The editors of the collection will make every effort to contact me to show me the final, edited version of my essay. I understand that by contacting Dr. Fellman at her office, I may change my mind about the inclusion of my essay if I wish.

Signature_____ Date_____

If my essay is used in the collection, I wish to be identified in the following manner *(please rank two choices)*:

Full name_____ First name only_____ First name+last initial_____
Initials only_____ Pseudonym _____

Biographical Information:
Birthplace_____ Gender_____ Race_____
Age: Under 21_____ 21–25_____ 26–37_____ 38–45_____ 46–_____
Marital Status_____ Children _____
ODU Student Number_____
ODU Status_____ Major_____ Minor_____
Career and educational goals_____
_____
_____
Class for which you are writing this essay:_____

Bibliography

Amster, Sarah-Ellen. "Anti-racist Education Makes the Invisible Visible." *Education Digest* 59.8 (April 1994): 21–24.

Asante, Molefi Kete, and Diane Ravitch, "Multiculturalism: An Exchange," *The American Scholar* 60.2 (spring 1991): 267–76.

Asch, Adrienne, and Michelle Fine, eds. *Women with Disabilities: Essays in Psychology, Policy, and Politics.* Philadelphia: Temple Univ. Press, 1988.

Bailey, Gerald D., and Nancy J. Smith. "Integrating the Effective Teacher and Sex Equity Literature by Developing Teacher-Made Process Materials." *Feminist Teacher* 2.2 (1987): 26–28.

Banks, Cherry A. McGee, and James A. Banks, eds. *Multicultural Education: Issues and Perspectives.* 2d ed. Boston: Allyn and Bacon, 1993.

Banks, James A. "Multicultural Education, Dimensions and Challenges." *Phi Delta Kappan* 75.1 (September 1993): 22–28.

———. *Teaching the Black Experience: Methods and Materials.* Belmont, Calif.: Fearon Publishers, 1970.

Belenky, Mary Field, et al. *Women's Ways of Knowing: The Development of Self, Body and Mind.* New York: Basic Books, 1986.

Biklan, Sari Knopp, and Diane Pollard. *Gender and Education.* Ninety-second Yearbook of the National Society for the Study of Education, Part 1. Chicago: NSSE, 1993.

Brandt, Ron. "On Educating for Diversity: A Conversation with James A. Banks." *Educational Leadership* 51.8 (May 1994): 28–31.

Brown, Lyn Mikel, and Carol Gilligan. *Meeting at the Crossroads: Women's Psychology and Girls' Development.* Cambridge: Harvard Univ. Press, 1992.

Butler, Johnella E. and John C. Walter, eds. *Transforming the Curriculum: Ethnic Studies and Women's Studies.* Albany: State Univ. of New York Press, 1991.

Campbell, Paul B., et al. *Outcome of Vocational Education for Women, Minorities, the Handicapped and the Poor.* Columbus, Ohio: The National Center for Research in Vocational Education, Ohio State Univ., 1986.

Cetron, Marvin J., and Margaret Gayle. *Educational Renaissance: Our Schools at the Turn of the Twenty-first Century*. New York: St. Martin's Press, 1991.

Cochran, Effiei P. "Giving Voice to Women in the Basic Writing and Language Minority Classroom." *Journal of Basic Writing* 13.1 (spring 1994): 75–90.

Crawford, Mary, and Margo MacLeod. "Gender in the College Classroom: An Assessment of the 'Chilly Climate' for Women." *Sex Roles* 23 (1990): 101–22.

Davidman, Leonard, and Patricia T. Davidman. *Teaching with a Multicultural Perspective. A Practical Guide*. New York: Longman, 1994.

Dublin, Thomas. ed. *Becoming American, Becoming Ethnic: College Students Explore Their Roots*. Philadelphia: Temple Univ. Press, 1996.

Dunbar, Paul Laurence. *The Complete Poetry of Paul Laurence Dunbar*. Edited by Joanne M. Braxton. Charlottesville: Univ. Press of Virginia, 1993.

Epstein, Debbie, ed. *Challenging Lesbian and Gay Inequalities in Education*. Philadelphia: Open Univ. Press, 1994.

Feiner, Susan F. "Introductory Economic Textbooks and the Treatment of Issues Relating to Women and Minorities." *Journal of Economic Education* 24.2 (spring 1993): 145–62.

Frankenberg, Ruth. *White Women, Race Matters: The Social Construction of Whiteness*. Minneapolis: Univ. of Minnesota Press, 1993.

Fraser, James W., and Theresa Perry, eds. *Freedom's Plough: Teaching in the Multicultural Classroom*. New York: Routledge, 1993.

Friedman, Marilyn. "Mathematics and the Gender Gap: A Meta-Analysis of Recent Studies on Sex Differences in Mathematical Tasks." *Review of Educational Research* 59 (1989): 185–213.

———. "Multicultural Education and Feminist Ethics." *Hypatia* 10.2 (spring 1995): 56–58.

Garcia, Karen. "Culture, Ethnicity, and Language for Puerto Rican Women." *Equity and Excellence in Education* 27.1 (April 1994): 34–36.

Gaudiani, Claire L., and Kelly R. Stern. "For a New World, A New Curriculum." *Educational Record* 75.1 (winter 1994): 20–29.

Giddings, Paula. *When and Where I Enter: The Impact of Black Women on Race and Sex in America*. New York: W. Morrow, 1984.

Gilligan, Carol. *In a Different Voice: Psychological Theory and Women's Development*. Cambridge: Harvard Univ. Press, 1982.

Glasgow, Joanne, and F. David Kievitt. "Outing the Classroom: A

Practical Guide." *Transformations: The New Jersey Project Journal* 5.2 (fall 1994): 28–35.

Grant, Carl A., and Christine E. Sleeter. *Making Choices for Multicultural Education: Five Approaches to Race, Class, and Gender*. 2d ed. New York: Maxwell Macmillan, 1994.

Grayson, Delores A. "Emerging Equity Issues Related to Homosexuality in Education." *Peabody Journal of Education* 64 (1987): 132–45.

Greene, Maxine. *Landscapes of Learning*. New York: Teachers College Press, 1978.

Hood, Marian White. "The Delta Team: Empowering Adolescent Girls." *Schools in the Middle* 3.3 (February 1994): 24–26.

hooks, bell. *Talking Back: Thinking Feminist, Thinking Black*. Boston: South End Press, 1989.

———. *Teaching to Transgress: Education and the Practice of Freedom*. New York: Routledge, 1994.

Hyde, Janet S., and Marcia C. Linn. "Gender, Mathematics and Science." *Educational Researcher* 18 (November 1989): 17–27.

Ihle, Elizabeth L. *Black Women in Higher Education: An Anthology of Essays, Studies, and Documents*. New York: Garland Publications, 1992.

Irvine, Jacqueline Jordan. *Black Students and School Failure: Policies, Practices and Prescriptions*. New York: Greenwood Press, 1990.

Lewis, Magda Gere. *Without a Word: Teaching Beyond Women's Silence*. New York: Routledge, 1993.

Marshall, Catherine, and Flora Ida Ortiz. "The Issue of Gender in Educational Enterprise." *Feminist Teacher* 2.2 (1987): 18–25.

McCormick, Theresa Mickey. *Creating the Nonsexist Classroom: A Multicultural Approach*. New York: Teachers College Press, 1994.

McKenna, Teresa, and Flora Ortiz, eds. *The Broken Web: The Educational Experience of Hispanic Women*. Claremont, Calif.: Tomas Rivera Center, 1988.

Morphew, Valerie N. "The Science Scavenger Hunt." *Science Scope* 17.6 (March 1994): 48–52.

Musil, Caryn McTighe, ed. *The Courage to Question: Women's Studies and Student Learning*. Washington, D.C.: Association of American Colleges, 1992.

NWSA Journal (Special Issue on the Feminist Classroom) 7.2 (summer 1995).

O'Barr, Jean, and Mary Wyer, eds. *Engaging Feminism: Students Speak Up and Speak Out*. Charlottesville: Univ. Press of Virginia, 1992.

Olivas, Michael A., ed. *Latino College Students*. New York: Teachers College Press, 1986.

Orenstein, Peggy. *Schoolgirls: Young Women, Self-Esteem, and the Confidence Gap.* New York: Anchor Books, 1994.

Pang, Valerie Ooka. "Why Do We Need This Class?: Multicultural Education for Teachers." *Phi Delta Kappan* 76.4 (December 1994): 289–92.

Pearson, Carol S., Judith G. Touchton, and Donna L. Shavlik, eds. *Educating the Majority: Women Challenge Tradition in Higher Education.* New York: American Council for Education: Macmillan, 1989.

Phelan, Patricia, and Ann Locke Davidson. *Renegotiating Cultural Diversity in American Schools.* New York: Teachers College Press, 1993.

Ravitch, Diane. *The Schools We Deserve: Reflections on the Educational Crises of Our Times.* New York: Basic Books, 1985.

Rosser, Sue V., ed. *Teaching the Majority: Breaking the Gender Barrier in Science, Mathematics, and Engineering.* Athene Series. New York: Teachers College Press, 1995.

Sadker, David, and Myra Sadker. *Failing at Fairness: How America's Schools Cheat Girls.* New York: C. Scribner's Sons, 1994.

———. "Sexism in the Classroom: From Grade School to Graduate School." *Phi Delta Kappan* 67.7 (March 1986): 512–13.

Sandler, Bernice, and Roberta Hall. *The Classroom Climate: A Chilly One for Women.* Washington, D.C.: Project on the Status and Education of Women by the Association of American Colleges, 1982.

Schoem, David L., et al., eds. *Multicultural Teaching in the University.* Westport, Conn.: Praeger, 1993.

Sidel, Ruth. *Battling Bias: The Struggle for Identity and Community on College Campuses.* New York: Penguin, 1994.

Stockard, Jean, and J. Walter Wood. "The Myth of Female Underachievement: A Reexamination of Sex Differences in Underachievers." *American Educational Research Journal* 21 (1984): 825–38.

The AAUW Report: How Schools Shortchange Girls. Washington, D.C.: American Association of University Women Educational Foundation and the National Education Association, 1992.

Thompson, Becky, and Sangeeta Tyagi. *Beyond a Dream Deferred: Multicultural Education and the Politics of Excellence.* Minneapolis: Univ. of Minnesota Press, 1993.

———. *Names We Call Home: Autobiography on Racial Identity.* New York: Routledge, 1995.

Weis, Lois. *Between Two Worlds: Black Students in an Urban Community College.* Boston: Routledge and Kegan Paul, 1985.

———. *Working Class Without Work: High School Students in a Deindustrializing Economy.* New York: Routledge, 1990.

Weis, Lois, and Michelle Fine. *Beyond Silenced Voices: Class, Race and Gender in United States Schools*. New York: State Univ. of New York Press, 1993.

Werner, Gabby, ed. *Just a Bunch of Girls: Feminist Approaches to Schooling*. Philadelphia: Open Univ. Press, 1985.

Winter, Suzanne M. "A Program for All Children." *Childhood Education* 71.2 (winter 1994): 91–95.

The Broad Minds Collective emerged out of a women's studies class at Old Dominion University. The collective was formed in 1993 to compile student self-portraits on cultural diversity and has stayed with the project until its completion as a book.

Kaaren Ancarrow worked on this collection while pursuing an MA in humanities with an emphasis in women's studies at ODU. Her thesis, titled "Transition or Tragedy: An Investigation of Cultural Attitudes Toward Women's Aging in the Literature of Menopause," reflects one of several women's health issues with which she is concerned.

Nan Byrne, a poet, lives in Virginia Beach with her husband Tom, and children Christopher, Jack Radovan, and Zoe. She teaches in the women and gender studies program at Virginia Wesleyan College and has recently completed work on a collection of poems, "Uncertain Territory," about mothers and daughters.

Jean Caggiano teaches speech at Hampton University and has also taught psychology at Commonwealth College in Hampton, Virginia. She is particularly interested in the concept of holistic health and is currently studying to become a massage therapist.

Anita Clair Fellman, the teacher in whose class the initial essays for this collection were written, is the director of ODU's Women's Studies Program and an associate professor of history. Her current research is on the place of the Laura Ingalls Wilder *Little House* books in American culture.

Brigita Martinson, an advocate for women's rights and children's health and welfare, has served as president of Friends of Women's Studies at ODU and is on the board of the Norfolk City Union of the Children's Hospital of the King's Daughters. She is working toward an MA in humanities at ODU and is currently pursuing her own consulting business dealing with human resources and fair labor practices.